Keys to Literacy for Pupils at Risk

LEE DOBSON

MARIETTA HURST

Pippin Publishing

Suite 232, 85 Ellesmere Road
Toronto, Ontario
M1R 4B9

Edited by Elma Schemenauer
Designed by John Zehethofer
Typeset by Jay Tee Graphics Ltd.
Printed and bound in Canada by Friesens

Canadian Cataloguing in Publication Data

Dobson, Lee
Keys to literacy for pupils at risk

(The Pippin teacher's library; 26)
Includes bibliographical references.
ISBN 0-88751-080-9

1. Language arts — Remedial teaching.
Language arts (Elementary). I. Hurst,
Marietta E. II. Title. III. Series.

LB1765.D62 1997 372.6'044 C97-931706-1

ISBN 0-88751-080-9

10 9 8 7 6 5 4 3 2 1

CONTENTS

FOREWORD

We are fortunate to have many enthusiastic and creative teachers as colleagues. We want to acknowledge May-ling Chow, who joined us in setting up a learning center for four- through thirteen-year-olds who were "at risk" of failing to become literate. We also wish to acknowledge Joy Nucich, who invited us into her ages four through eight classroom to team-teach. The four of us collaborated in 1991 in writing the Language Arts Curriculum which appears in *Whole Language: Practical Ideas*.

Jean Kotcher observed and made audiotapes of our interactions with pupils in the Learning Center and in classrooms. This research formed the data for her 1989 thesis, *Teaching Literacy Through Interaction*. Jean's records enrich our book and we thank her for making them available to us.

Keys to Literacy for Pupils at Risk highlights the key role teachers play in their interactions with pupils. Teacher-pupil dialogues are at the heart of the book as they are at the heart of teaching.

We wish to express our gratitude to the many other colleagues who supported the development of our program. They include Maureen Brady, Shirley Brunke, Asako Chan, Rachel Duncan, Chuck Jordan, Lynda Stickley and Beth Trask.

INTRODUCTION

Early in our careers, when we were classroom teachers, we noticed that there were always pupils who were falling farther and farther behind. They seemed to have a number of problems. Some were learning English as a Second Language. Some had experiential gaps. Some faced physical, mental or emotional challenges which interfered with learning. Regardless of the source of their problems, they were "at risk" of failing to become literate.

To pursue our interest in such pupils, we attended post-graduate courses. We became Learning Assistance Teachers in a school for pupils aged four through ten. We worked with a school-based team consisting of classroom teachers, the principal, a psychologist and a counsellor to identify at risk pupils. Then it was up to us to put together an appropriate program.

Initially we taught at risk pupils on a withdrawal basis following standard diagnostic and teaching procedures. But we were unhappy with the results. Too often our pupils were apathetic and discouraged. They were reluctant to engage in the assigned tasks. We wanted them to become confident and keen learners.

Therefore, we investigated the latest research and identified new theories which focused on the development of language, literacy and thinking. We tried new approaches and carried out our own research, which was published in 1985. We forged new practices which accelerated pupils' progress and changed their whole attitude to learning. These results renewed our energy and joy in teaching.

We moved to a larger school, teaching at risk pupils aged four through thirteen. Many were learning English as a Second Language. We continued to withdraw pupils for lessons but also joined classroom teachers to team-teach. We found that the strategies we applied in the Learning Center worked equally well in mainstreamed classrooms.

As we consolidated our program, we began to give demonstrations, conduct workshops and teach education courses at the University of British Columbia. We offered private tutorial sessions to learners of all ages in a variety of settings. We continued to reflect further on our work and refine our teaching.

We have set out our program and its underlying principles in *Keys to Literacy for Pupils at Risk*. We invite you to join us in the classroom, where we draw out the connections between practices and the theory that supports them. We explain why and how we proceed as we do. Listen in as we relive and share our coaching sessions. The pupil-teacher interactions we report stem from our records and those of Jean Kotcher.

Our studies led us to establish a cohesive set of principles which ground our program for pupils at risk.

Principles

1. Provide a warm social setting in which pupils feel safe to take risks and reveal their thinking.
2. Immerse pupils in a literate environment and invite them to participate in reading and writing.
3. Expect pupils to choose materials and topics for themselves so they can pursue purposeful reading and writing.
4. Look through pupils' reading and writing to identify learning strategies.
5. Respond to the meaning in pupils' reading and writing as the absolute priority.
6. Treat hypothesis testing and self-correction as evidence of thinking.
7. Respect pupils' functional creations of reading and writing.
8. Recognize and coach pupils' development along a learning continuum.
9. Evaluate progress individually and over time.

In the first three chapters of this book, we present keys to understanding reading and writing and how they develop.

While we present reading and writing in separate chapters, we emphasize that these aspects of literacy intertwine and interact at all times.

In the following chapters we present keys to developing effective interactions with pupils. If you practise using the strategies you will find they become second nature—they are powerful strategies that work in mainstreamed classes, special classes, ESL classes, Learning Centers and extra sessional clinics.

The final chapters set out the reading and writing programs. They provide you with keys to identify pupils' strategies, to evaluate their effectiveness, and to individualize programs. We hope the ideas contained in this book will benefit you and help *you* reach *your* goals.

KEYS TO UNDERSTANDING READING

Pupils at risk approach reading in various ways. Some are afraid to risk error, and are unaware of the strengths they have. Some are impatient with analyzing print. They fill in gaps in their minds or gloss over inconsistencies. Some are engrossed with the mechanics and miss much of the meaning. Some have excellent comprehension even if they read laboriously. Some read with a nice balance of strategies and good expression, but actually understand little. Pupils at risk need support in integrating all the strategies.

We can observe and analyze pupils' strategies as they read. They use three language cue systems: the syntactic system, the semantic system and the graphophonic system. They bring their background knowledge to the task. They work to integrate this knowledge as they use the cue systems to make sense of their reading.

The Cue Systems

All readers make errors or miscues which are the alterations readers make to the text. These aren't harmful incidents. As Ken Goodman pointed out in 1972, they provide a window on the patterns of strategies readers use. Writers' errors provide the same opportunity.

Miscue analysis, as explained by Yetta Goodman and Carolyn Burke in 1972, enables us to examine how pupils are using the cue systems during reading. We can pose questions which help us to observe reading at these levels of language.

THE SYNTACTIC CUE SYSTEM

The syntactic cue system consists of a complex set of internalized language rules which allow children to predict and generate the grammatical sentences of their language. In English these include the use of aspects such as word order, parts of speech and inflections or affixes which alter the grammar of a sentence.

Observe pupils' miscues at the sentence level. What are they doing with grammatical aspects?

- Do they change the grammar of the sentence?
- Do they create a grammatical sentence or part of a sentence?
- Do they notice when a sentence doesn't sound right? How much do they rely on the grammatical cue system?
- Do they rely on their sense of grammar to correct miscues?

THE SEMANTIC CUE SYSTEM

The semantic cue system comprises the system or set of meanings which children organize in terms of their own experiences, vocabulary, concepts and conceptual structures. When print stands alone, language becomes the sole context on which readers can rely.

Observe pupils' miscues at the sentence level. How are they using semantics?

- Do they change the meaning of the sentence?
- Do they create a meaningful sentence or parts of a sentence?
- Do they notice when their reading doesn't make sense?
- Do they rely on meaning to correct miscues?

THE GRAPHOPHONIC CUE SYSTEM

The graphophonic cue system comprises the complex set of relationships between patterns of letters in print and patterns of sound in speech. These occur at the word level. Readers synchronize two sets of sequences—of print in space to sound in time. They combine information on the look and sound of words.

Observe how your pupils are using the graphophonic cue system.

- Do they follow the conventional layout of print; from left to right, and from the top of the page to the bottom?
- Do they read words as units?
- Do they use graphophonic cues to predict the wording?
- Do they use the first letter as the main clue?
- Do they produce nonwords?
- How much do they use the graphophonic cue system?
- Do they use this system to correct miscues?

INTEGRATION STRATEGIES

Pupils at risk use the same cue systems as proficient readers. And they use them simultaneously. It is the integration and combining of information from the cue systems that they find most difficult. They need to bring all their background knowledge and strategies together to predict and monitor their efforts. They develop this integration by reading with the larger picture in mind. They learn to read by reading.

Observe the integration strategies that pupils are using.

- Do they bring their background knowledge to the task?
- Do they use predicting and confirming strategies?
- How are they combining strategies from other cue systems?
- Do they use them in balance?
- Is there a pattern to their strategies?
- Do they have a repertoire of strategies?
- Do they read fluently?
- Are they aware of the strategies they are actually using?
- Do they choose to read in their free time?

Observing Reading

You can observe the cue systems pupils are using, beginning by audiotaping an oral reading. Then document the reader's miscues, or alterations to the text, on a printout of the text. Use the Miscue Code which is on page 12.

Miscue Code	
Little	an underline marks a rereading
want won't	cursive script above, marks a substitution
some / milk	a slash line marks a hesitation
it	a circle marks an omission
by it ^ myself	a caret locates the insertion written above
C cookies eggs	an underline with c marks a successful correcton

Vicki is seven years old and reading aloud in her second language. Marietta is sitting beside her. To recreate Vicki's reading, translate the coded text on page 13 of *Little Red Hen,* written by June Melser in 1980. Keep in mind her use of the cue systems and their integration.

Analyzing Reading

Consider each miscue across the cue systems.

In miscue #1 on line #4, Vicki substitutes *cookies* for *eggs,* producing the question *Who will get me some cookies for the cake?* She is creating a grammatical sentence. But does her miscue make sense at the sentence and story levels? Little Red Hen might want to serve cookies along with the cake, but isn't likely to want cookies *to make* the cake. It also doesn't fit immediately after saying *I will make a cake.* So semantically, Vicki is making sense at the sentence level, but not in the context of the story. As *cookies* neither sounds nor looks like *eggs,* Vicki isn't using a graphophonic cue to predict the word. Both graphophonic and semantic cues at the story level prompt her to correct the miscue.

In miscue #2 on line #5, Vicki substitutes *want* for *won't,* reading, *"I want," said the cat.* The miscue is a very close

CODED TEXT OF VICKI'S READING OF *LITTLE RED HEN*

1. Little Red Hen
2. Little Red Hen lived with a cat and a rat and a mouse.
3. Little Red Hen said, "I will make a cake."
4. "Who will get me some eggs for the cake?"
5. "I won't," said the cat.
6. "I won't," said the rat.
7. "I won't," said the mouse.
8. "Then I will get them myself," said Little Red Hen.
9. So she did.
10. Little Red Hen said, "Who will get me some flour for the cake?"
11. "I won't," said the cat.
12. "I won't," said the rat.
13. "I won't," said the mouse.
14. "Then I will get it myself," said Little Red Hen.
15. So she did.
16. Little Red Hen said, "Who will get me some milk for the cake?"
17. "I won't," said the cat.
18. "I won't," said the rat.
19. "I won't," said the mouse.
20. "Then I will get it myself," said Little Red Hen.
21. So she did.
22. Little Red Hen said, "Who will help me make the cake?"
23. "I won't," said the cat.
24. "I won't," said the rat.
25. "I won't," said the mouse.
26. "Then I will make it myself," said Little Red Hen.
27. So she did.
28. "And who will help me eat the cake?" said Little Red Hen.
29. "I will," said the cat.
30. "I will," said the rat.
31. "I will," said the mouse.
32. "No, you will not," said Little Red Hen.
33. "You will not help me eat it.
34. I will eat it myself."
35. So she did.

graphophonic match. A regular phonetic spelling of *want* would be *w-o-n-t*. Both words are verbs. The sentence is potentially grammatical up to the point of the miscue, but an object should follow the verb *want*. After several repetitions of this miscue, Marietta asks Vicki to explain her understanding. She replies, "They want different things." Vicki is putting her own interpretation on the story. When she adds her own object to the verb, she also makes it sound right.

Vicki meets the same phrase on line #11. This time she substitutes *I what* for *I won't*. Her immediate dissatisfaction with *I what* seems to come from the mismatch in grammatical functions. This miscue distorts the meaning as well as the grammar. The look and sound of *what* and *won't* are similar, which suggests Vicki is trying to use graphophonic cues. When Marietta asks her to think what else it could be, Vicki is able to self-correct.

Miscue #4 on line #14 suggests the influence of Vicki's limited experience with English. She omits it, leaving the sentence as *"Then I will get myself," said the Red Hen*. Vicki often omits prepositions in her speech. This isn't a reading concern because she is translating the reading into her own words.

In miscue #6 on line #21, Vicki substitutes *And she did* for *So she did*. In miscue #8 on line #28, she substitutes *the red hen* for *Little Red Hen*. In both instances she predicts a grammatical and meaningful sentence. Yet she notices the miscues and self-corrects. She is using a graphophonic strategy to cross-check and correct her predictions.

The detailed description and discussion above provides a great deal of information. But we need to organize and collate it into a manageable form before we can analyze Vicki's strategies. For this purpose we use a Miscue Record, based on those originally described by Yetta Goodman and Carolyn Burke in 1972. Here is a procedure you can follow to fill in the Miscue Record.

On the coded text, number up to 25 miscues (the alterations a reader makes to the text). This gives a sufficient number to reveal the pattern of strategies in a reading. Skip over miscues that are exact repetitions of ones already numbered. These offer no new information, and might distort the results.

Miscue Record

Name Vicki
Date
Selection Little Red Hen

	Text	Reader
1.	eggs	cookies
2.	won't	want
3.	won't	what
4.	it	—
5.	Little Red Hen	the red hen
6.	So	And
7.	make	do
8.	Little	the
9.	—	by
10.		

Miscue Record

Did the miscue —

	1 rely on graphophonic cues?			2 keep sentence grammar?			3 keep sentence meaning?			4 keep story meaning?		5 get corrected?		6 either keep story meaning or get corrected? = yes	
	2/3	Part	No	Yes	Part	No	Yes	Part	No	Yes	No	Yes	No	Yes	No
1			✓	✓			✓				✓	✓		✓	
2	✓				✓			✓			✓		✓		✓
3		✓				✓			✓		✓	✓		✓	
4	—	—	—		✓			✓			✓		✓		✓
5			✓	✓			✓			✓			✓	✓	
6			✓	✓			✓			✓		✓		✓	
7			✓	✓			✓			✓		✓		✓	
8			✓	✓			✓			✓		✓		✓	
9	—	—	—	✓			✓			✓		✓		✓	
10															
Total	1/7	1/7	5/7	6/9	2/9	1/9	6/9	2/9	1/9	5/9	4/9	6/9	3/9	7/9	2/9
%	14	14	72	66	22	11	66	22	11	56	44	66	33	78	22

Then move on to the Miscue Record. Fill in the introductory section on the first page. In the *Text* column, note the first text word or phrase which the reader has altered.

In the example of Vicki's reading, fill in *eggs* on the first line. Across from it, in the *Reader* column, note miscue #1, *cookies*. In the same way fill in *won't* in the *Text* column and *want* in the *Reader* column. For the omission in miscue #4, fill in *it* in the *Text* column and put a dash in the *Reader* column. For the insertion in miscue #8, put a dash in the *Text* column and note *by* in the *Reader* column. When you've finished listing the miscues in this fashion, move on to the next section.

The second page of the Miscue Record guides us to examine each miscue across the cue systems. It prompts us to ask questions as we fill in the columns from left to right.

Does the miscue:

1. rely on graphophonic cues? *Yes* (2/3), or *Part* (1/3), or *No* (none)?
2 create either a fully or partially grammatical sentence?
3 create either a fully or partially meaningful sentence?
4 preserve or keep meaning consistent with the story?
5 get corrected?
6. *either* keep the story meaning *or* get corrected?

In column #1, *graphophonic cues,* analyze the words in approximate thirds. If two-thirds or more of the word is similar in look and sound, give credit in the *Yes* column. If only one-third is similar, fill in the *Part* column. Leave column #1 blank for omissions (miscue #4) and insertions (miscue #9), because they have no graphophonic features.

In column #2, *keep sentence grammar,* decide whether a reading produces a sentence which is either fully or partially grammatical. If it is only partial, mark the *Part* column. Keep in mind that a sentence might be grammatical even if it doesn't make sense.

Fill in column #3, *keep sentence meaning,* on a similar basis. In column #4, *keep story meaning,* decide whether the reader significantly alters the meaning of the story.

In column #6, summarize the significant information from columns #4 and #5. Put *Yes* in column #6 if there is a *yes* in either column #4 or #5. Thus if the miscue is *either* consistent with the story as a whole *or* gets corrected for meaning, the reader gets credit for making sense of it.

Total the columns and compute the percentages. In the example, Vicki scores only seven miscues in the *graphophonic cues* column because of the omissions and insertions. She scores nine in the others.

Vicki makes full use of graphophonics at 14%, partial use at 14% and no use at 72%. She preserves the sentence grammar at 66%, makes partial use at 22% and no use at 11%. She uses the semantic system in the same proportion.

Look at the balance in Vicki's use of the cue systems. She keeps the miscues consistent with the meaning of the story at 56%. She corrects 66% of her miscues, and fails to correct only three (33%). The last column indicates that Vicki retains or corrects the meaning in 78% of her miscues.

The Miscue Record illuminates Vicki's control of some key strategies. She uses all the cue systems to predict, but she mainly relies on meaning and grammar. This represents an imbalance. However, when the meaning is disturbed she makes good use of graphophonics to cross-check and correct. Therefore, she is integrating strategies to solve problems while keeping the larger picture in mind.

Coaching Priorities

We have established a progression of key priorities in coaching reading, in order to focus our observations and expectations on pupils' specific needs. The order of priorities matches the order in which pupils usually control these aspects; of course pupils will be working on a number of priorities at once, but control tends to come in that order. Our highest priority will vary accordingly as it helps us to individualize coaching appropriately.

The key coaching priorities are:

1. to coach pupils to engage in and enjoy meaningful reading.
2. to coach pupils to integrate strategies with a sense of the whole.
3. to coach self-correcting strategies.

4. to coach for a balance in the cue systems.
5. to coach strategies for choosing suitable reading material.
6. to coach pupils to develop independent strategies in learning to read.

We can easily check how Vicki is doing in terms of these priorities. She is controlling the first three priorities and is engaging in and enjoying meaningful reading. She is integrating strategies with a sense of the whole, and is using self-correcting strategies. She is working on the fourth priority of using the cue systems in balance. This, now, becomes our coaching priority.

Vicki has fulfilled the fifth priority of choosing suitable reading material. She chose *Little Red Hen*, which has a straightforward plot and a strong storyline. The language is memorable with its rhythm and refrain. These features allow Vicki to work on the balance of her strategies. The Miscue Record shows she is handling her choice well. Therefore, the selection is very suitable at this stage of her learning. We will keep a watchful eye on Vicki's continuing control of this priority.

As Vicki refines her strategies, she is also becoming an independent reader—the last priority. As her control increases, we will check to see if she needs encouragement to challenge herself with more difficult material.

The Miscue Record evaluates strategies during reading. But to have a full evaluation, we must also determine what a pupil retains and comprehends after a reading. Vicki's retelling and discussion will confirm that she comprehends well and spontaneously relates the theme to her own life.

The Miscue Record is time-consuming to do in detail, but it provides us with a qualitative perspective of reading strategies. With experience, we come to recognize the strategies simply by listening to pupils reading aloud. Then we reserve the Miscue Record for a detailed diagnosis.

The reading profiles of pupils at risk vary considerably. When we analyze pupils' reading, we discover which strategies they control and which they need to develop further. Then we can individualize our coaching according to their priorities.

KEYS TO UNDERSTANDING WRITING

Pupils at risk bring a wide range of experience and understanding to learning to write. Some have had many satisfying encounters with writing while others have had few. They vary in their experience of the special characteristics of written language, the structures and conventions of different genres, the workings of the graphophonic cue system and their understanding of the process as a whole. Pupils at risk use the same strategies as proficient writers. They know when something makes sense or sounds right. What they find most difficult is to integrate all these aspects into their writing.

Proficient writers use several sets of strategies as they write. These strategies involve cue systems at three levels of language: the syntactic, the semantic and the graphophonic. Proficient writers effectively integrate these cue systems.

We can analyze how pupils are using the cue systems. However, it is difficult to look across the cue systems as we did in reading. In writing it is more effective to consider each system separately before looking at the piece as a whole.

The Cue Systems

The following description of the cue systems includes questions we can pose to help us observe writing in detail during the process and after its completion.

THE SYNTACTIC CUE SYSTEM

The syntactic cue system in writing employs the word order, the parts of speech and inflections that readers use. It also uses additional conventions, such as spaces between words and punctuation marks, as clues to intonation and pauses. Young writers incorporate these grammatical aspects according to their understanding and awareness of them.

Look at pupils' sentences and consider what they are doing with the grammar.

- Are pupils creating grammatical sentences or parts of sentences?
- Does their writing take on characteristics of written grammar or sound like talk written down?
- What punctuation are they using?
- Do pupils notice grammatical errors while writing or rereading their writing? Do they try to solve any problems? How?
- Do they read with a sense for sentences when the punctuation is missing?
- Do their grammatical errors reflect their speech?

THE SEMANTIC CUE SYSTEM

The semantic cue system comprises the system or set of meanings which young writers communicate in terms of their own experiences, vocabulary, concepts and conceptual structures.

Look at pupils' sentences and consider how they are using semantic cues.

- Do pupils write fluently enough to record their ideas or do transcription problems interfere?
- Can they sustain writing? Can they put down, resume and complete writing?
- Do they reread as they write, to retain or reestablish their trains of thought?
- Does the writing make sense? Do they notice when it doesn't? Do they correct for meaning as they write and after they have finished?
- Can readers make sense of their writing?

THE GRAPHOPHONIC CUE SYSTEM

The graphophonic cue system in written English comprises the complex set of relationships between patterns of sound in speech to patterns of letters in print. Young writers apply their judgments and familiarity with letter/sound connections to transcribe their compositions.

Consider how pupils are using graphophonic cues.

- — Do they set out their writing conventionally—from left to right, and from the top of the page to the bottom?
- — What phonetic strategies do they use to spell unfamiliar words?
- — What visual strategies do they use?
- — Do they represent grammatical suffixes on a phonetic basis?
- — What spelling conventions do they generalize?
- — Are the words readable by them and others?
- — How fluently do they transcribe their thoughts?
- — Do pupils ask for help or resolve their own problems?
- — What errors do they notice as they reread their writing?
- — What corrections do they provide or attempt?

INTEGRATION STRATEGIES

Proficient writers draw on all their experience and understanding in their writing. They combine strategies from the three cue systems and integrate them to suit their purpose and anticipate the needs of their audience. Pupils at risk tend to find it difficult to be flexible, to manipulate various aspects of the language consciously and to integrate the strategies.

Consider the integration strategies pupils are using.

- — Do they choose to write for their own purposes?
- — Do they write for a variety of purposes? Do they choose the structure accordingly?
- — Do they anticipate readers' responses and needs?
- — Do they consider the effectiveness of the piece as a whole?
- — Is the writing logical, organized and cohesive?
- — Do pupils edit during and after writing? How? At what levels of language?
- — Do they elaborate in writing? How?
- — Can they insert missing information?
- — Are they aware of language as an entity to manipulate?
- — Do they proofread for meaning, grammar, wording and spelling?

Observing a Piece of Writing

Leo was nine years old when he wrote the first draft of his story, *the maci ston*. An analysis of the writing follows the example. While you read Leo's story, think about the cue systems he is using.

The maci ston
Once upon a time ther was
a very nice Old man he gave
the kids in the arkaed money
to play more vedo games
if he got a shoe shin and if
it was brety good he gave
them 50¢ More becaues he was
rich and because all he wanted
was a boy of his on then
One day he was in the forst
wen he saw a maci rock
then the rock became a
maci wising ston in riling
it said it will give you
three ~~tothe~~ wishis so frist he
wishis for One boy ~~to~~ then

he went home and put
his son to sleep and thohg
if it wistax for -
Ten 1000! son ill be famos
ass well ass rich! so ~~tricht~~
a # Qick so I wish ~~it~~ for 70.000
Sons and then then stod
all then ten 1000 of them
and because it was the yer
1960! so he was so happy
to see them he wished for
a limo to sid in but it had
Ten 1000. sets
then he
thothg OH NO now I can not
have onuf food for this

Kids

OH Boy! I Don't know about this
Smidley! POW!POP!Pam!
showy! wabab SSSSSSsss!
shhhhhhhhhhh! PPPPPPPPPPPP-
ppppPPPPP-# WOOOOOOO!
POW!!!!!!!!
and all the this stof he
wished for was gon!

Analyzing Writing

THE SYNTACTIC CUE SYSTEM

Leo's composition sounds mostly like a written story. He uses complete sentence structures and includes the complexities of relative and conditional clauses.

Leo consistently writes from the third-person perspective of the storyteller, using the past tense to relate events. He switches appropriately to the present tense, and uses the first-person *I* to report what the stone said in writing and to relate the old man's thoughts. Then he maintains these structures for an extra sentence before returning to the third-person, past tense.

While Leo composes with a tacit or unconscious sense of sentence, he transcribes without marking most sentence boundaries. He does, however, locate a number of exclamation marks appropriately.

He conventionally represents the grammatical suffixes *-ed* and *-ing*. He notices and crosses out the third-person ending of *wishes*, which does not agree with *I*. The corrected sentence reads, *If I wish for 10,000 sons I'll be famous as well as rich!* If you heard Leo tell the ending of the story, *all the this stuff he wished for was gone*, it might sound fine. The word *the* occurs in an unstressed part of the sentence, so you don't really notice it. But when we read the same sentence, we notice the problem.

THE SEMANTIC CUE SYSTEM

Leo's choice of vocabulary is generally specific, but it includes some informal terms, such as *stuff, kids* and *limo*. His writing is generally readable and makes sense. However, the lack of sentence demarcations makes it difficult to recapture.

The cross-outs indicate that Leo often corrects for meaning. Yet it's hard to make sense of one section which translates into *so a Qick so I wish for 10,000 sons and ther then stood all then ten 1000 of them and because it was the year 1960!* The sketches in the body of the text provide important details that are not in the writing.

THE GRAPHOPHONIC CUE SYSTEM

Leo's many correct spellings tell us little. But we can examine his strategies by looking at the errors.

Leo's phonetic approximations make most of his words quite readable, as in *wen, riting, shin, ston, gon, onuf* (enough) and *stof*. The spelling of *wishis*, in *three wishis*, suggests that he is focusing on the sound rather than the grammatical function of the suffix *-es*.

Visual strategies are at work in irregularly-spelled words such as *becaues, thohg, thothg* (thought) and *maci* (magic). Leo uses most of the necessary letters, but sometimes writes them out of sequence.

Leo works on generalizing various conventions. His spelling of *arcade* as *arkaed* indicates his awareness that two vowels can work together. When he spells *pretty* as *brety*, his use of *y* represents another convention.

INTEGRATION STRATEGIES

Leo's piece integrates many elements that are typical of written stories. It contains a clear beginning, middle and end. It uses conventional wording to open the story and introduce the main character. It sets up and temporarily solves the story problem. Its use of magic, three wishes and *Once upon a time* are characteristic of fairy tales.

While Leo's readers could admire the imagination and action of the story as a whole, they would want to know a number of details about the man and his son. They would also want to know how all the *stof he wished for* disappeared at the abrupt conclusion of the story.

Coaching Priorities

Let's establish a progression of key priorities in coaching writing in order to focus our observations and expectations on pupils' specific needs, and enable us to individualize coaching appropriately. Their order matches the order in which pupils tend to control these aspects:

1. engage in and enjoy meaningful writing.
2. write more fluently.
3. use self-correcting strategies.

4. consider the need to expand and elaborate writing.
5. choose suitable topics which they know and care about.
6. develop independent strategies in learning to write.

We can easily check to see how Leo is doing in terms of these priorities. In this piece of writing, Leo fulfils part of the first priority. He is engaging in meaningful writing. He seems to be operating from an intuitive awareness of grammar and the elements of a story. His inclusion of sketches suggests that while he has more ideas, he finds it too laborious to transcribe them. Leo is unlikely to enjoy writing while it takes so much effort.

Leo is still not writing fluently. He needs to work on this second priority before he can make much progress on later ones. He is doing some self-correcting, but there is little evidence of rereading, editing, expanding or elaborating his writing. With fluency he will find it easier to develop a sense of the whole, and will then see the purpose to reviewing writing.

Leo has partially fulfilled the fifth priority of choosing a suitable topic which he knows and cares about. His story has the structure and much of the language of a fairy tale. It is meaningful, which suggests that he does care about it. He seems to control the genre, but his knowledge is at an intuitive level. He is not at the stage of thinking about the structure and language to suit his purposes.

This analysis evaluates one piece of Leo's writing after its completion. It tells a great deal about his use of the cue systems. It doesn't examine his strategies during writing, nor does it consider his responses to coaching. A full evaluation would include diagnostic teaching during and after writing.

The writing profiles of pupils at risk vary considerably. When we analyze pupils' writing individually, we discover which strategies they control and which they need to develop further. Then we can personalize our coaching according to the priorities.

THE DEVELOPMENT OF GRAPHOPHONIC STRATEGIES

All pupils learn literacy by forming increasingly sophisticated hypotheses of how reading and writing operate. They create a series of rule systems which are systematic but unconventional. As they revise their rule systems, their reading and writing more closely approximate conventional literacy.

Emergent writing is the period from which pupils first attribute meaning to their writing representations until they achieve a graphophonic match that others can read. Emergent reading is the period from which pupils first attribute meaning to books or print until they integrate their predictions with graphophonic strategies.

Emergent readers and writers generally know when something makes sense or sounds right. They know least about the graphophonic system. They learn by forming and testing hypotheses for using graphophonic strategies within the whole process.

Therefore, it is vital to recognize, observe and encourage their progress within the whole. Although this chapter highlights pupils' use of graphophonic strategies, their use is in the full processes of emergent writing and reading.

There is abundant research demonstrating that graphophonic strategies develop along a continuum of learning. The researchers observed and described the continuum in stages, and that's what we'll be doing in this chapter, using the labels provided by Richard Gentry in 1982: the precommunicative, the semiphonetic, the phonetic and the transitional.

Graphophonic Strategies of Emergent Writers

We will first observe the strategies of emergent writers. We will analyze what they are doing rather than what they are not. While we will discover many regularities in development along the continuum, we need to watch out for individual differences.

THE PRECOMMUNICATIVE STAGE

At this first stage, children represent writing in some form. They may use scribbles, symbol-like or letter-like forms, or random numbers and letters. They start to attribute meaning to their writing representations.

Once pupils recognize the time/space match between the message and the print, they work to create and retrieve it. They may reuse some print, add more print, or compose more to achieve a match. We can observe their strategy by asking them to read with a finger.

THE SEMIPHONETIC STAGE

At the semiphonetic stage, children use letters to represent sounds. They begin with a partial mapping which gives the writing a telegraphic character. Pupils first write in letter strings without spaces between words. During this stage, most children stabilize the left-to-right orientation, although they often reverse letters for some time.

Pupils may start with captions or a short phrase. For example, Molly writes *HFN* and reads it as *Hi, friend*. Molly's example is typical of this stage. She transcribes the most distinct features of words in a letter string. These are the consonant sounds and the beginnings and ends of words. She also uses the more distinct forms of letters which are usually the upper case.

Tom writes a longer message which is more difficult to retrieve. The italicized letters indicate the matching points of the message he reports.

iWTTMKZPLSADHWgt
*I w*ent *t*o *m*y cousin's *pl*ace *a*n*d h*e *w*as *g*ood.

Tom's transcription is typical of semiphonetic writing. He represents many consonants and few vowels. He prints the lower case *i*, which is the more distinct form of the letter. The upper case *I* is similar to lower case *l* and the numeral *1*.

Tom's choice of *t* to represent the last sound of *good* is systematic. He is following a rule which is common to emergent writers but unconventional in adult terms. He bases his analysis of sounds on where he articulates them in his mouth. The sounds /d/ and /t/ come from the same part of the mouth.

Some children find it difficult to retrieve the match they create. If they predict a paraphrase, they may find it frustrating and confusing to reread their writing. But early matches are significant events to discover and support. Observe pupils carefully during writing so you can provide the encouragement and support they need at this fragile stage.

Pupils use letter names or their approximations as cues to the words or word parts they represent. Jillian uses the common letter-name strategy, choosing *U* to represent *you* when she writes:

INoU
I know you.

Children use a number of these representations, such as *Y* for *why* and *r* for *are*.

When Jillian represents *know* as *no* she is overgeneralizing its spelling. It makes good sense, but is unconventional. Such overgeneralizations indicate pupils are looking for patterns, forming hypotheses and applying systematic rules.

The segmentation of words makes them more readable. It marks a significant advance in learners' understanding of the graphophonic system.

Some pupils begin to segment by using punctuation marks. Graham says that he uses dashes "so *they* don't go into each other."

A-HTETATE-HAS
A haunted house.

Shirley's example illustrates a common strategy at this stage. She knows she needs to use spaces, but forms her own rule of where they go. She overgeneralizes segmentation as being at the syllable level, rather than at the word level.

TR WZ A BT A FL HS

There was a beautiful house.

Two weeks later, Shirley adapts her rule to incorporate the concept of word segmentation:

TR WZ A BTAFL PEStD
There was a beautiful present.

In this example, Shirley makes the common omission of a nasal (*n* or *m*) before a consonant. She writes *present* as *PEStD*. She bases this judgment on the place of articulation in her mouth.

THE PHONETIC STAGE

At this stage, learners start mapping most of the sounds they perceive. Examine Don's example:

Wan Saponatayme Dar Wows A cat and
Dar Wows A dog the doG Sapt on the cat and the cat
Wows Fat and the cat Dayd

Once upon a time, there was a cat and there was a dog. The dog stepped on the cat, and the cat was flat, and the cat died.

Don demonstrates several features of this stage. He uses *D* as an approximation of his pronunciation of the sound of *th* in *there*. He uses vowels in appropriate places, but often not the conventional ones. He also omits part of two blends in *Sapt* for *stepped* and *Fat* for *flat*.

Don represents the past tense in terms of the sound of the suffix. He prints a *t* in *Sapt* for *stepped*. While he segments most of his words conventionally, he finds some common phrases, such as *Once upon a time*, confusing.

THE TRANSITIONAL STAGE

Pupils at the transitional stage transcribe more easily and start incorporating visual strategies. They use an increasing number of conventional spellings and start to take irregular spellings into account.

Vicki writes the following piece at about the same time as she reads *Little Red Hen*.

One day I want oet Saed it was so so so drak thet I can't Blevete. it was so drak and wned to thet I can't Blevete.

One day, I went outside. It was so so so dark that I couldn't believe it. It was so dark and windy too that I couldn't believe it.

Vicki is still working on her concept of a word, as in *Blevete* for *believe it*. She is using conventional spellings, such as *one, day, was* and *can't*. She is beginning to incorporate visual aspects, as in *oet* for *out* and using two vowels in *Saed* for *side*. Vicki's writing is becoming more readable as she moves out of the emergent writing stage.

Vicki uses graphophonic strategies extensively in her writing. She does much less analyzing in her reading of *Little Red Hen*. In a 1989 book, Lee Dobson showed that most pupils apply these strategies in writing before they do in reading.

Pupils at risk progress along a learning continuum in their development of graphophonic strategies, and our familiarity with this continuum enables us to individualize our coaching appropriately.

Graphophonic Strategies of Emergent Readers

Initially, children rely on context to predict the meaning of print. The context resides in the setting of a printed sign, the illustrations of a favorite book, or the drawings that accompany their writing.

Pupils gradually realize that print holds the meaning and wording. They discover there is an arbitrary direction to follow in transcribing and reading writing. They slow down their message to match the units of print they track. They resolve mismatches of the units in a variety of ways.

In the following example, Shirley manages the difficult task of matching words unit by unit to the first line, while inventing a storylike opening, "There was a monster." On the second line, she abandons the print and creates her own story.

There was a monster.
Where are they going?

The wizard looked at the silly monsters.
Look! Here is a wizard.

On that same day, Shirley writes and retrieves the following message:

TW-AMSLD
There was a magical land.

The difference in strategies between Shirley's reading and writing is typical of pupils at this stage. Although she uses semiphonetic matches in writing, she is only working at a time/space match of word units in her reading of unfamiliar stories.

Children use different strategies to read familiar stories. They use the language and wording they remember.

When Marietta presents Shirley with the memorable and familiar book *Brown Bear, Brown Bear*, written by Bill Martin, Jr. in 1970, she dips in and out of the print and achieves a number of word-perfect matches.

A big brown bear.
Brown bear, brown bear, what do you see?

Bear big brown bear big brown bear what do you see?
Brown bear, brown bear, what do you see?

I see a redbird
I see a redbird looking at me.

Redbird, redbird, what do you see?
Redbird, redbird, what do you see?

I see a yellow duck yellow duck, yellow duck
I see a yellow duck looking at me.

What do you see
Yellow duck, yellow duck, what do you see?

I see a blue horse
I see a blue horse looking at me.

b) Blue horse
a) What do blue horse what do you see
Blue horse, blue horse, what do you see?

At this point, Shirley self-corrects from *What do* (a) to *Blue horse* (b), and then stays with the print. Then for four pages she emphasizes word units and reads accurately, except for the recurring phrase *looking at me*. Then she comments, "I just turn a few pages—so it won't be so long, right?"

After skipping four pages and the occasional word, she adds a new strategy of repeating the previous refrain to stand for the problem phrase. She maintains this strategy, reading more rapidly to the end.

I see a teacher I see a teacher.
I see a teacher looking at me.

Teacher, teacher, what do you see?
Teacher, teacher, what do you see?

I see kids I see kids.
I see children looking at me.

Kids, kids, what do you see?
Children, children, what do you see?

Two weeks later, when Shirley reads an unfamiliar book, *A Monster Sandwich*, which Joy Cowley wrote in 1983, she returns to her strategy of invention. While she abandons the graphophonic strategies she used in *Brown Bear, Brown Bear*, her comments indicate she is cross-checking some predictions with the print:

Text	Reader
A monster sandwich	The cheese store
A monster sandwich	One day Jenny and Thomas went out.
	"Oh, God, nothing starts with J."
Put some lettuce on it.	A lettuce sandwich is good for you.
Put some cheese on it.	My best is Swiss cheese.
	"Ah, it starts with c."
	(Sounding *s-w-is*.)

When pupils start to cross-check and self-correct their predictions with graphophonic cues, they are taking significant steps. They are beginning to integrate graphophonic strategies into their reading. This is the very aspect that pupils at risk find most difficult, but we can encourage and support pupils as they work through this fragile period, helping them to keep a sense of the whole while they develop graphophonic strategies.

In the following four chapters, we highlight and illustrate key elements in our interactions with learners. These interactions embrace the heart of literacy learning and teaching pupils at risk.

. . . .

MEANING

We read to discover and construct meaning. We write to crystallize thought and convey meaning. We must keep these purposes in the forefront when coaching pupils at risk. Our first priority is for pupils to engage in and enjoy meaningful reading and writing.

Emergent readers do not have the graphophonic knowledge to read conventionally, but we still expect them to select a book and produce a sensible reading. Notice the knowledge and strategies that Graham, a kindergarten pupil, brings to the following reading.

Graham (G) selects a small, eight-page book called *Go, Go, Go*. He opens it and begins to "read" to Marietta (M).

G: I know that one is G. And that's the first name of Graham. (He points to the print in the title.)
M: Say how it goes. Say what's in your head.
G: I'm trying to think. (He looks at the illustration.) Let me see...what that fox is doing. I'll try and think what that fox is doing so then I'll know.
M: Tell me what's in your mind.
G: You know what all I can get in my mind is?
M: What is that?
G: Only the words.
M: What are the words?
G: Let me see. Can I turn the page? ...I'm not very good at thinking.
M: I think you are.
G: A bit good. (He looks at the illustration.) All I can think about is a cat and the owl in the pea green boat.
M: Hmmm.

G: (He turns three pages.) Now I should start. Hey! *X-O-X*. (He identifies the print on a vat.)
M: What are you thinking now?
G: Now, let me see what the words are. Hmmm. "Stop hopping, Mama." And Mama's saying, "I can't stop hopping. We have to meet Daddy. Remember?"
M: So you did have a good thought, after all.
G: Only on the last page.

Graham's first focus is on the print. He recognizes some letters and relates them to his name. Then he looks to the illustrations for cues, and tries to think what the words might be. One picture suggests a familiar story, *The Owl and the Pussycat*, but he realizes this isn't the same. Finally, he uses another illustration to create a humorous and meaningful piece of dialogue.

Throughout, Marietta guides and extends Graham's responses. She listens intently and replies with interest and encouragement. She emphasizes the need for him to think and to convey his thoughts. She builds on his responses and asks for elaboration, but doesn't supply any new information. The result is a gradually emerging picture of Graham's knowledge and strategies.

Regardless of handicap or disability, all children are trying to make sense of their worlds. They ask why, hypothesize reasons for this and that, and watch for routines and patterns. Observe their strategies. Encourage them to do what proficient readers do—use prior knowledge and experience to predict meaning.

Coaching Meaningful Reading

Some children recognize a few letters and words. They identify some sound-letter correspondences. But they view reading as a passive occupation, and don't work to integrate their strategies to create meaning. Robert is one of these. Lee is his teacher, and her challenge is to set up situations which actively engage him in meaning-making.

Lee starts to build a collection of all the words he can read. First, she asks him for suggestions, prompting him to remember names of family and friends. Then she takes him on a "hall walk" in the school to see if there are signs such as *BOYS* and *OFFICE* that she can add to the list. Under his watchful eye, she prints each word he knows on a card and gathers them into a pile. She prints *Yes* and *No* on separate cards and hands them to Robert.

Lee (L) explains that she will use the cards to form sentences. She wants Robert (R) to read the sentence and put down his *Yes* card, if the sentence makes sense, or his *No* card, if it doesn't. She begins with the sentence *Robert is a boy*.

R: Robert, is, a, boy. (He reads haltingly.) Yes. (He places his *Yes* card on the table.)
L: Good reading. You are a boy. (She reshuffles the cards and forms *Robert is a girl*.)
R: Robert, is, a, girl. Yes. (He places the *Yes* card on the table.)
L: Read it again.
R: Robert, is, a, girl. Yes.
L: Are you a girl?
R: No, I'm a boy!
L: You're sure?
R: (He nods vigorously.)
L: Well, think what the sentence says.
R: Robert / is / a / girl. Oh! Robert is a girl. No! I mean no! (He scrambles to put the *No* card in place.)

After a number of successful responses, Lee changes roles. She gives him the pile of words and asks him to form sentences. She will respond "Yes" or "No." This new challenge encourages playing with words. His enjoyment is obvious as he sets up nonsense sentences.

Once a pupil like Robert becomes eager to participate, we add new procedures. For example, we use the cards to form messages such as "Go to the office." They read and follow the instructions. Then they form the messages and we follow their orders.

We introduce the occasional "mystery" word. These are words we don't expect pupils to recognize at sight. If possible, we place these words at the ends of sentences, so that pupils can use the beginnings for their predictions. Those who rise to the challenge and figure them out are well on their way to becoming readers.

Russell (R) is a pupil at risk, but he is older and seems more proficient. Lee (L) listens as he reads his chosen book. She notes his fluency and expression. Then she moves the book away.

L: Now, tell me about the story in your own words.
R: I need.... (He moves his hand toward the book.)
L: No, without the book. Just tell me the story.
R: I, I, I, I don't know.
L: Think back over the story. Who was in the story and what happened? Tell me about it.
R: Well, there was a dog...and a cat, I think.

This is all Russell seems to remember.

Further investigation reveals that he can use the book to locate answers. This strategy and Russell's fluent reading encourage people to think that he is a capable reader, but he does not remember, think about, or interpret meaning. When he is expected to discuss text, he is lost.

Closely monitor the independent reading of such pupils. Have them read one paragraph or a short page of text, and then close their books and tell about them. At times you may ask, "Have you ever had an experience like that?" or "Why do you think that happened?"

As pupils become more able, lengthen the intervals between the interruptions. But continue to expect them to talk about their ideas. Discussion motivates pupils like Russell to search for and retain meaning.

COACHING DURING READING

Our second priority is to coach pupils to integrate strategies with a sense of the whole. When they falter in their reading, we pose questions like, "Does that make sense?", "What would make sense?" or "What does it mean?"

Marietta (M) initiates the following dialogue when Diane (D) stops reading at the word *begging*.

D: The animals were..., animals were, were....
M: Okay. Tell me about that. What do you understand? What about the animals? What is he doing? (She points to an elephant in the illustration.)
D: (An inaudible mumble.)
M: What does he want?
D: Peanuts.

M: Have you ever heard of what you say when pets are showing that they want some food? What do we call it? What are they doing?

D: Hungry.

M: They are hungry. But we say they are doing something. It's like they're asking for food. Only they can't use language. They can't say, "I am hungry." So, what do they do?

D: They...bark?

M: They bark; yes. It's a kind of speaking. Sometimes they might show what they want without barking. What is it that they are doing, in fact? Can you think of a word that describes it?

D: Begging?

M: Could that be? Try it with the print.

D: (Reading from the book:) The animals were begging for peanuts.

M: Now, just pause for a moment. You have worked that out for yourself. I didn't have to tell you what the word was. How did you do that?

D: (Pointing:) 'Cause this is begged.

M: Well, how did you know that?

D: It has to be a *b*.

M: It does, but you also figured it out from the picture, the story and from what you know in your head. Good thinking!

Marietta begins with general questions which draw attention to the meaning in the text and illustrations. When Diane doesn't respond, Marietta becomes more specific. Her cues gradually build up the context until Diane predicts "begging." Marietta does not confirm this answer, but suggests Diane decide whether it is appropriate. Marietta's final statement reinforces Diane's use of the illustrations, plot and prior knowledge as sources of meaning.

If pupils have problems, help them identify the source. Use their knowledge and endeavors as a base for comments and questions. Stress their ability to find and apply their own solutions. Then ask them to explain their thinking. At a later session, you may remind them of their successful strategies.

Readers must expect what they read to make sense not only in the context of the selection, but in terms of their own life experiences. Encourage them to place their own interpretations on a selection and to decide what its significance is.

Kenny (K) reads the story *Jack and the Beanstalk*. Then he tells the story to Marietta (M). In the dialogue which follows, Marietta asks questions which help Kenny express his own views of the matter.

M: What a long story you told. You are out of breath. So, what was the real problem in the story?
K: Jack and his mom wanna be rich. Wanna be rich.
M: Yes; right. And did someone learn a lesson?
K: The Big One.
M: What did he learn, the Big One?
K: I don't know. I think he don't kill people. I don't know.
M: Well, think about it for a moment. What might he have learned?
K: Don't get mad at the little people. The little persons...the children..., because they only a little kid.
M: Oh, what a nice thing to learn. Do you feel that sometimes in your own life? Can you tell me of a situation like that?
K: Oh! I forgot.
M: When you are saying don't hurt the little people?
K: Yeah! The little kids.
M: Have you had a problem with that?
K: Sometimes.
M: Yes; what happens?
K: Well, if you kill these little children, they'll be dead and they have to learn the lesson *Don't kill the little people.*
M: Don't kill the little people.... That's quite a lesson. We could all take a lesson from this story. Do you ever put a lesson into your stories?
K: I don't know.

With this hint for future writing, Marietta ends the session.

Probe for pupils' ideas and feelings about the specific problems and lessons in a story. Then lead them to relate their own experiences. When pupils have problems putting their ideas into words, help them by supporting and clarifying their efforts. When you are sure they have said all they can, you may summarize or paraphrase the ideas before winding up the discussion.

Coaching Meaningful Writing

Pupils write meaningfully when they write from their own knowledge and experience. To obtain this goal, we coach them to choose their own topics, and help by asking those who are already writing to share their topics and their stories. We encourage discussion and inquire how others might address similar topics. We suggest they retell favorite stories and poems, and make the setting a safe place in which pupils can reveal and relive their lives.

COACHING DURING WRITING

We do not become too involved at the pre-writing stage, because we don't want pupils to use our ideas rather than their own. If they are stuck, we suggest drawing a picture or explaining their ideas orally. However, the discussion must not become a substitute for writing. We say to pupils, "That sounds interesting. But don't tell me any more. Write it down, and I'll read it when you're through. Don't worry about the spelling or punctuation. Just write what's in your mind."

Marilyn (M) draws a picture first, and then tries out titles for her intended story. Lee (L) sits nearby, seemingly occupied in other work. Marilyn talks, mostly to herself, as she thinks and writes.

M: Okay. The rabbit and the mice and the cat. No. I want the rabbit and the mice. No, a tortoise. ...Okay?
L: A tortoise. Good idea!
M: Tortoise...tortoise.... The rabbit and the tortoise and the dog.
L: Uhmmm.
M: One day, ...the rabbit.... One day, the rabbit asked the tortoise...tortoise and the dog ...dog for a race... (She is writing.)

L: Good for you! (She glances at Marilyn's book.)
M: ...in the park....
L: Uhmmm.
M: The rabbit said, "Ready, said..."
L: "Ready, set?"
M: "Ready, set, go." And...I was going to put it backwards—*A-D-N*. That's not a word; that doesn't make sense. *A-N-D*.
L: Good correcting!
M: And the dog...sleep.
L: Uhmmm.
M: "Ready, set, go." And then the dog sleeped.
L: Oh! It's the dog that's sleeping!
M: "Ready, set, go." And then the dog sleep...for one hour, hour, hour; where's my hour? *H-O-U-R*...for one hour, and then, then I think...I think he'll sleep....
L: Uhmmm. So, the dog sleeps for one hour; and then?
M: And then.... And then....
L: I'm wondering what these other animals are doing. (She points to the illustration.)
M: The rabbit won! And...then...the...rabbit asked the tortoise. (She continues to write.)

We stay close to children like Marilyn who need help to keep their writing on track. We may assist with special vocabulary, such as the idiom "Ready, set, go." However, we don't offer new information. We help writers over the rough spots by reading their last words and asking "And then?" or reminding them of the characters and situations in their drawings. We want to help pupils recover and extend their original ideas.

RESPONSES TO PUPILS' WRITING

Respond to the meaning in pupils' writing. If you are unsure of their intentions, read between the lines. Then ask for confirmation and clarification. Your interest will often motivate writers to extend their pieces.

Jason draws a picture of two smiling people. One of them is standing on one foot, with the other foot up off the ground. Underneath he prints:

today my Fads yaze plag raslg

The following episode begins with Jason (J) pointing to each word in turn, as he reads his message to Lee (L).

J: Today, my friends was playing wrestling.
L: Oh! Is this one of your friends, kicking with his foot? (She points to the picture.)
J: Yes, and he is playing.
L: Does he trip people with his foot when he's wrestling?
J: Yeah, and they, they fight; and, you know, they have to throw them down, and the other one have to count, and when they count the other one win.
L: Oh, so if I get somebody down and count....
J: No, the other one count. 1 2 3.
L: Oh, there is a referee.
J: Yeah, and he counts up to three, and when he does, that guy wins.

Lee asks Jason about his drawing so she can understand his writing. She gets some clarification, but realizes his language problems. So, she changes her focus from drawing out information to refining what has been offered. When she puts herself into the action, she discovers one of the problems: he is unfamiliar with, or can't remember, the word "referee." Once she supplies it, Jason uses a rather complex grammatical structure to clearly describe the situation.

Jason is experiencing difficulty at many levels of language. He needs encouragement to communicate his meaning in pictures as well as in writing. Then we can respond to the total context of the printed message and illustration. Our focus is on clarification, not correction. And as this example indicates, this is often enough to motivate pupils to make significant improvements.

Pupils learn as they write and discuss. Each experience adds to their repertoire. A successful literacy program is grounded in meaning. It nurtures existing knowledge and strategies, encourages reflection and creates a motivating environment for writing, reading and learning.

. . . .

RESPECT

Respect is a major catalyst in language learning. Parents naturally accord their children great respect in learning to understand and speak. When two-year-old Nick says, "Me cookie!" to his mom, she doesn't stop to correct him, but responds to his expected intention by replying, "Of course; here you are." Parents expect children to succeed simply by immersing them in purposeful language. They unconsciously focus on what children can do, applauding the smallest indications of progress, and providing endless enthusiasm and feedback. They respect the meaning behind all attempts. Consequently, children pursue language with great gusto, full of confidence that they can learn through their own efforts.

When we accord pupils respect for the understanding, competence and strategies they possess, we make exciting discoveries. This setting enhances the opportunities to use our expertise to coach literacy.

Observing to Promote Respect

We observe, recognize and respect Kate's competencies as she approximates the "Big Book" of 1982, *Who Will Be My Mother?* by Joy Cowley.

Text	Reader
Lamb went to the rabbit.	———
"Rabbit, rabbit, will you be my mother?"	"Rabbit, rabbit, will you be my mother?"
"I am a rabbit," said the rabbit.	"I am a rabbit," ———
"I can't be your mother."	"I can't be your mother."

Lamb went to the bull.	———
"Bull, bull, will you be my mother?"	"Bull, bull, will you be my mother?"
"I am a bull," said the bull.	"I am a bull," ———
"I can't be your mother."	"I can't be your mother."

Kate's emergent reading incorporates significant strategies. She knows where to open a book and which way to turn the pages. She matches the timing of her reenactment to the illustrations. Although she is a young ESL pupil, she is working on different levels of language all at once. In spite of omissions, she recreates the complete meaning of the story and much of the exact wording. Her rendition is totally grammatical. Kate is using her strengths and working on integrating them into the whole. And she orchestrates this complex task fluently, with no reference to the print! She is reading with expression and obvious satisfaction, making sense of reading. Reading is complicated, yet Kate clearly sees herself as a reader!

Programming to Promote Respect

EXPECT PUPILS TO CHOOSE THEIR OWN TOPICS

Learning to write is a function of experience. Pupils learn to write by writing. The more regular and frequent the writing, the more rapid the progress. When pupils choose their own topics and teachers respect their choices, writing becomes genuine and, therefore, worthwhile. Not all teachers believe that this theory works in practice, as we see in the following situation:

> Freda is a university student who is planning a writing lesson. She intends to introduce it with a story that is expressive of feelings. After a discussion, she expects the pupils to choose and write on their own topics dealing with feelings. But faculty and classroom advisors warn her against this plan. They explain that some pupils in the class regularly refuse to write—her lesson won't be successful. Despite this advice, Freda believes students will find writing purposeful if they believe the communication of ideas is the priority. She decides to persevere with her plan.

All but a core group of three start to write quite readily. Freda approaches the three, pointing out that this is a first draft, and they shouldn't worry about such details as spelling and handwriting. She stresses her interest in what they have to say. They can write about an experience in the past, a situation in the present, or even an event that might happen in the future. Hans, the group leader, asks, "Can I write about taking a driver's test?" When Freda says he can, Hans begins to write. Then Tony and Quon follow suit. Tony's first draft follows.

The irrisponsible idiot?

He seemed like a very irrisponsible
Person, he would not do his
homework, because he was
not interested in it but
everybody else thought he
was just wasting his time
doing other things, but
he wasn't really wasting
his time he was just not
interested in his work
but he was really quite
Smart but nobody Knew
that because he wasnt
very interested in the
work he was assingned

Tony shows his inexperience in his immature printing, the omission of sentence markers and overgeneralization of commas. Yet his spelling is quite conventional, and the grammatical structure is fairly complex. He chooses a purposeful message and expresses it with feeling. His willingness to try and to risk error are worthy of respect.

The question mark in Tony's title is a meaningful touch! Not only does the "irrisponsible idiot" seem smarter than he lets on, but so does the writer. Pupils are willing to show their true abilities when they care about the topic and know teachers will respect what they have to say.

EXPECT PUPILS TO COMMUNICATE MEANINGFULLY

The confidence of Jasmine, a young ESL child, shines through the following piece of writing, where she encourages her friend Cindy to try.

> One day I went Outsid withe my frands at the park and we had fun and I was sweeng on the sweeg and I told sindy cumon get on the sweeg But I am skard and She got on the sweeg and She said I can sweeg and we all went houme if you tri thigs and ouer skard just tri them and you feel that you are a stor

> One day, I went outside with my friends at the park, and we had fun, and I was swinging on the swing. And I told Cindy, "Come on, get on the swing." "But I am scared." And she got on the swing, and she said, "I can swing!" And we all went home. If you try things and are scared, just try them, and you feel that you are a star.

Jasmine is willing to show both her weaknesses and her strengths. She chooses a topic from her own experience. She has the confidence and control to convey her lesson about life. She sees herself as a writer. She is a writer.

SEARCH FOR PUPILS' COMPETENCIES

Marietta (M) is listening to James (J) as he reads aloud from Joy Cowley's *The Sunflower That Went Flop.* Observe her responses to his attempts to make a meaningful reading.

J: (Reading:) The *sunflower* was hot and... ("No.") ...The sun was hot and days passed. One afternoon, the sunflower suddenly went flop. *What a shame,* said the people passing by. *Mrs. Brown,...it's, it's* ***had*** *it....*

("Wait, wait. I gotta read it; read that thing before I read it out loud.")

M: Oh, okay.

J: *What a shame,* said the people passing by....

M: Uhmmm....

J: *Mrs. Brown,...it's....* ("Uh, I don't know that word. I gotta try the rest of the sentence.") *It's...it again,* she said.... *It's* ***done*** *it again!*

M: Good. That was an excellent strategy. What worked so well when you got stuck?

J: I read it again.

M: Yes! And it worked. That's often a good thing to do. But you found even more good things to do. You read around that tricky word and then used your good thinking to find a word that made sense!

J: Oh, yeah!

M: So, what can you try when you're stuck?

J: I can read around it.

M: Exactly!

James is monitoring and correcting his reading, so Marietta respects his efforts. She resists the impulse to help or correct him. She supports him by saying, "Oh, okay." and "Uhmmm." James stops himself when his reading doesn't make sense, and corrects his miscue of *sunflower* for *sun*. He pauses again when he notices his second miscue, *had* for *done*. James tries again, but is still stuck, so he skips the word and completes the sentence. He then returns and corrects the miscue. Afterward, Marietta asks James to reflect on his successful strategies.

Pupils need to develop monitoring and self-correcting strategies. They learn these within the complete process. James' running commentary shows that he is aware of potential problems and of strategies for their solution. When Marietta asks him to review what he has done, she is extending this awareness. Children often give little thought to their strategies. But they gain confidence when they realize what they are doing right! Even though they have fallen behind their peers in learning, they can reflect on and solve their own problems.

Respect your own expertise to evaluate pupils' efforts. Focus on what they can do; recognize and accept their levels of competence. Don't patronize students by giving false praise; give them a positive but honest view of themselves. Respect is a major key to literacy.

. . . .

CONTROL

It is human nature to assert control. Pupils must gain active control of reading and writing to integrate the various cues. This is how they become literate.

Yet we neither leave learners to stumble on their own nor give them the opportunity to opt out. We give them as much independence as possible, while supporting their developing strategies. We ask them to assume increasing control, but keep watchful of situations where they need their coaches back at their sides.

Learning to Read

To develop control, pupils need ready access to a large collection of quality literature which must be able to spark the interest of pupils with a wide range of ability. Then they can learn to choose material which they can understand and enjoy.

We provide worthwhile, readable material, so that reading may be genuine. Compare the language from two versions of a folk tale.

1. *The Gingerbread Boy*
   "No!" said Gingerbread Boy.
   "I'll not come to you.
   I'll run away from you."

2. *The Gingerbread Man*
   He said,
   "Run, run,

as fast as you can.
You can't catch me—
I'm the gingerbread man."

These versions support quite different views of how pupils learn to read. The language in the first example contains a limited number of high-frequency words. The language in the second example is natural and predictable, and it uses rhyme, rhythm and refrain. Which is more readable?

Current wisdom supports the second version. The language just flows. Children treat it as a favorite, and delight in choosing to read it over and over. They find it purposeful, genuine reading. They control it.

Control of Reading

Sam chooses a book from the classroom library. It is an illustrated book that describes what loggers do. Marietta (M) listens to Sam (S) as he reads aloud. When Sam hesitates, the following exchange occurs.

M: You noticed something! See if it makes sense. Start again.
S: (Reading:) *We have to **sell** these logs down the river to the mill.*
M: Does that make sense? To sell these logs down the river to the mill? ... Okay. Where do you think the problem lies? Think it through.
S: Sawed?
M: We have to what?
S: Sawed.
M: Sawed. *We have to **sawed** these logs down the river to the mill.* Hmmm. What do they have to do with these logs? Forget about the print. Just explain it to me. Use your picture clues, too. What do the men have to do?
S: They cut them down. They put them in the water.
M: Yes.
S: They cut them up.
M: Yes. So, what happens in the water, then?
S: They, um, the logs; they pull them down the water.

M: That's right, they have to tie them together in these log booms so they can pull them with the tug boats. So you've understood. Great! Keep reading.

Marietta begins by commenting about an event that might seem dysfunctional—a hesitation in reading. But hesitations often signal thinking, so she lets Sam know that it's a good strategy to follow up. She suggests he reread the sentence to provide time to think and to keep the full context available.

When this advice is insufficient, she repeats the essence of the sentence and asks whether it makes sense to him. He responds with a single word: *sawed*. Sam has located the problem word. Marietta reads the beginning again, leaving it for Sam to continue. When he doesn't respond, she shifts the focus by asking what he knows about logging. Now he can concentrate fully on the meaning.

Once Sam demonstrates his understanding, Marietta tells him to carry on with his reading. Cues at the word level form just part of the reading process. While Sam is still unable to predict the particular word *send*, he certainly understands its meaning.

We must not lead pupils to abandon promising, yet often fragile, strategies of monitoring and creating meaning. Take the responsibility of using your knowledge of the reading process.

Reading non-fiction draws on background knowledge of structure, style and the complexity of written language. It often involves abstract concepts and specialized language beyond readers' understanding.

Ensure that pupils have the necessary background to make sense of their reading. If they don't, encourage them to choose other books. If they want to do research, provide suitable material.

Hesitations often signal the presence of a crucial strategy: monitoring understanding while reading. Pupils use cues from many sources to cross-check their predictions. Observations and discussions reveal which strategies are within their control, which they are picking up on their own and which they can work on with support.

Keep pupils in control while observing how they monitor and cross-check their predictions. Use your observations to coach them toward independence.

Learning to Write

We are all communicators. Infants communicate meaning even before they can speak—there is meaning behind all their communications. Children readily assign meaning to their writing efforts, whether they are readable or not; they may simply have to interpret what they write. The communication of meaning makes writing genuine.

Assigning topics may seem to make writing easier, but it does not. Suggesting or assigning topics leads pupils to believe their own experiences are mundane and invalid.

Declare your faith in pupils' ability to choose their own topics and write meaningfully. Expect them to be in control of their own compositions.

Control of Writing

Kenny (K) brought a problem to Marietta (M). Kenny was in the process of writing about robbers who steal money. The leader of the good guys is *Leader One*. Kenny wanted an alarm to alert the good guys. The following discussion took place.

M: Tell me in your own words.
K: He heard it flash on.
M: How could he hear it?
K: It made a noise.
M: Did you write that? See if you can figure it out.
K: No, it's not here, and I don't know if I can figure it out—where to put it.
M: Tell me more. (She covers the writing with her hands.)
K: Leader One saw a red light.
M: Tell me what he heard.
K: A red buzzer flashed on.
M: Ahhh, very good!
K: A red buzzer flashed on. (He mutters to himself as he writes.)
M: You worked it out beautifully—*A red buzzer flashed on.* I can hear it and I can see it.

Marietta places her initial priority at the semantic level. She asks Kenny to concentrate on what he wants to say. When he says, "It made a noise," she thinks he has solved his problem. But he hasn't. She redirects his attention to what he wants to say. Then he easily completes the insertion.

Marietta works from the general to the specific, but finds she has shifted ground prematurely. Separating transcription from composition allows Kenny to resolve his problem. The objective is to give pupils no more help than is necessary. Marietta provides the need and opportunity to develop problem-solving strategies. The least teaching is the best teaching; pupils must learn how to learn.

Rob (R) moves to the big city just before school opens in early September. His first day in the resource center is at the end of the month. Rob brings his work to Marietta (M); he has a tidy drawing with neat printing underneath:

I saw a cat
Sat.

Rob initiates the conversation:

R: I've finished my story.
M: Great! Will you read it to me?
R: *I saw a cat sat.* (Reading hesitantly and word by word.)
M: Oh! Is he your cat?
R: Yes, and he's black, just like I drawed him.
M: Mmmm. He's beautiful. I see he's sitting outside this house.
R: Yes. But don't you like my printing?
M: Yes, of course I do. You do nice printing.
R: (Rob smiles proudly.)
M: Rob, tell me about the house.
R: It's my house; my new house. But he's scared, 'cuz he doesn't know his way, yet.
M: Are you scared, too? It's scary coming to a new school, isn't it?
R: Yes, but now I come to school with Angelina. She's in my class.
M: That's nice, isn't it? Rob, why do we write?
R: The teacher wants us to.... So we'll learn.
M: Yes, that's true. But, it's what you are trying to say that counts. You've just told me a lot of things that are special. I wonder what you'll write about tomorrow? I bet I'll be surprised.
R: Okay. See ya tomorrow.

Marietta places total priority on the meaning. She encourages Rob to elaborate on the information in his writing and drawing. When he interrupts her agenda by asking whether she likes his printing, she acknowledges it. However, she quickly steers the conversation back to the meaning. When Marietta asks Rob to tell her about the purpose of writing, he confirms her fear: he is writing to please his teacher, and is only working on part of the process. Rob doesn't see his writing as making meaning or communicating his ideas. He's not in control.

Rob knows what he can do well at the surface level. He restricts himself to words he thinks he can spell correctly, and focuses his effort and pride on his printing. Yet Rob converses easily about things that are significant to him. Marietta ends the conversation by emphasizing the priority on communication over mechanics.

The next day, Marietta (M) heightens the focus on meaning by asking Rob (R) what he is going to write about. He says he is going to write about his mom and dad. He draws a careful picture of a man and a woman by a house. He starts to write slowly, and stops after a short while. Marietta notices and comes to talk to him.

I Love my mom
and DaD

M: Read me what you've written so far, Rob.
R: I love my Mom and Dad....
M: Hmmm.
R: That's all I have in my family. We all came here.
M: How nice. Yes, I love my mom and dad, too.
R: Everybody does.
M: Right. How come?
R: 'Cuz. They are important.
M: Yes, they sure are. I'll come back to see you, when you've finished.

This time, Rob chooses a topic he cares about, yet his wording suggests he's still playing safe. By asking him to elaborate orally, Marietta hopes to nudge him into expanding his writing. She quickly leaves him alone to support her expectation that he can write more. And he does!

Bcs
th r im prt

When Marietta returns, Rob reads the whole story.

M: Ahhh, yes; I can read that, too. I love my mom and dad because they are important.
R: Yes, and my cat and dog, too. (He picks up his pencil and adds the rest.)

and cat
and boc

By reading the writing herself, Marietta is emphasizing its value and readability. She consciously places the entire focus on his message.

From then on, Rob immersed himself in writing with a sense of control that he had yet to experience in reading. When he wrote *th r im prt* for *they are important,* his writing was genuine. Rob only needed a little encouragement to break out of the prison of correctness. Marietta could immediately see his level of control over composition and transcription. Then she knew how to coach him.

Pupils like Rob need to be convinced that you really mean it when you tell them not to worry about spelling. Then they will feel safe to show their true level of competence. Don't try to shield them from making errors. That is not to suggest they do whatever they like—far from it. Coach learners to take responsibility for monitoring and correcting their own work. Such control sets pupils firmly on the path to independence.

ACCOUNTABILITY

We coach pupils to develop independent learning strategies. This means they must become accountable to engage in reading and writing. Some may feel such activities are beyond them. But even beginning readers can use illustrations to predict meaning; they can represent their ideas in drawings, symbols or letters. We expect pupils to engage in any way they can, and to be ready to explain their intentions. We observe, encourage, support and share their endeavors.

Choosing What to Read and Write

We coach pupils to choose suitable reading material. Pupils at risk usually don't have experience choosing their own books, so they may feel uncertain and ask for help. We may say, "Take your time. Look through the books and find one you want to read. It's up to you."

We accept their choices. But if they decide their books are unsuitable, we ask them to reflect on their strategies. We say, "Tell me about your choice," and "What are you going to do differently, when you choose again?" Then we leave them to choose and try other selections.

We coach pupils to write on suitable topics in terms of their interests and knowledge. If they say they have nothing to write about, you may respond, "Well, I remember just yesterday you were telling me something about....Write your ideas down, and then they will be there for people to read." or "This is a time when you can write what you have to say. You can write about what you have done and what you are thinking about. Don't worry about spelling or anything like that. Just write in any way you can."

Sometimes pupils choose topics they don't really care about. Roger (R) is an example. He is a confident reader, but seldom chooses to write.

Lee (L) approaches as Roger sits gazing at a title he has written at the top of a page.

L: Now, is this the topic you want to write on? That's the first question.
R: What topic?
L: Your title. Is this what you want to write about?
R: It is. (He says this somewhat belligerently.) This is the topic.
L: Uhmmm. Well, I am wondering, because it is hard to write something if you really don't care what you are saying.
R: Yeah!
L: You see, you have got to want to write about the title you choose.
R: Can I change?
L: Sure, sure. You want to write a story that you want to write. It has to be yours. That's what I'm saying.
R: (After a pause:) Miz D., I really don't feel like I want to do this. I have to think.
L: You've got to think about it. Well, okay. I think that's a good idea. Get a book, read it, and tell me about it when you are finished reading.

Lee challenges Roger's commitment to his topic. Then she leaves the issue for him to think about, but she doesn't relax the expectation that he will write. The sequel to this session follows:

> When Roger returns a few days later, Lee tells him to find a nice, quiet place to write. He sits at an empty table, but just stares at his open folder. After a few minutes, she reminds him that it is important not to try to be too perfect, and to just start writing. Once she turns her attention elsewhere, he gets up and wanders around. He looks sad, discouraged and vulnerable. At the book table, he flips through some books. He calls over his buddy, Roy, and together they start to look at books. Lee comes over and says, "I don't know why you two

> are finding it so difficult to write." She adds, "I am getting irritated at waiting for this writing." There is little reaction from the boys. Finally, she says, "We'll all write together."
>
> She goes to her desk, gets her personal folder and joins Roger and Roy at a table. She says, "Now we're all going to write. I've got something to write, too." And she begins. Roy watches her curiously, and says something. She looks up at him and says, "You are interrupting me. I don't want to be interrupted while I am writing. You have your own work to do." Roger looks very bewildered. Lee continues writing. She occasionally pauses and looks up, clearly thinking about what she is doing. Roger twists around to look at others at an adjacent table. He leans on his arms and watches his buddy, who is writing. He gets up, goes to the supply table and comes back with an eraser. He watches Lee intently. She looks up, but does not meet his gaze. Roger picks up a pencil. By now, twenty minutes have passed. More children start to filter in. Lee is still composing, and Roger finally starts to write. He writes a bit more, then erases. He rests his chin on his hand, looks around, writes some more, erases and writes. There is no talk at this table, although the rest of the room is humming with activity.

If pupils don't settle down to write, we may sit at the same table and begin our own writing. We are trying to create a setting in which we are comrades striving to reach a common goal. Our unspoken message is "I believe you can do it by yourself, just as I can. I don't need to help you." But at the same time, we are modeling the required behavior.

Don't let engagement in writing become a struggle between you and your pupil. Make it an ordinary, everyday activity.

Engaging in Writing

Some children have a great deal of difficulty with transcription. They may have immature spelling strategies or omit punctuation, but they are still accountable for writing. We don't give up on them, and we don't allow them to give up on themselves.

John just sits. He makes little effort to get his ideas onto paper. Rather than confront him with his lack of work, Lee says, "John, I know you're finding it hard to get started. It is rather noisy and distracting in this room. Why don't you take your work and write in the room across the hall? It's empty right now. You'll find it easier to work there."

John looks at her and almost immediately begins to write. This is his piece as written:

avre bute has mor paprs but
I haveun gust frey af I b
t rit i haftu go an a rom
bimislf and i hatay rit and
i dod lik fat and fas the ind
a the store

John reads his writing to Lee as follows. When you match his written and spoken versions, you will discover strengths as well as problem areas.

Everybody has more papers, but
I haven't—just three. If I
don't write, I have to go in a room
by myself and I have to write, and
I don't like that, and that's the end
of the story.

Lee responds, "Good for you. You really can write here, even though it's a bit noisy."

We can understand John's feelings of inferiority and his sensitivity to the suggestion that he write in a room by himself. We can see his difficulties but also his strengths. He writes the truth as he perceives it, and thus demonstrates an understanding of what writing is all about. The piece reveals his voice as a writer. Lee doesn't intend to be harsh, but she does expect John to write, and he finds he can.

Engaging in Reading

Readers are accountable for producing a meaningful reading. If something doesn't make sense, we expect them to notice and attempt a correction. If they do not, we step in and question their interpretation.

In an earlier example, James (J) read Joy Cowley's 1982 story, *The Sunflower That Went Flop* to Marietta (M). Here he continues the reading.

J: Mr. Brown opened up his fix-it bag and got out some sticky tape. *This should do it,* you said.... No, *he...he said* (correcting himself). He went sticking, sticking, sticking and stood the flower up by the well again. What a

M: Excuse me. Is there a well? Or am I hearing you correctly?

J: Well? ...Wail?

M: Are we talking about a well?

J: Yeah!

M: Is the sunflower by a well?

J: No, by the

M: What do you think it's by?

J: Wood!

M: Uhmmm! I can see something made of wood in the illustration, but I'm not sure that

J: A fence! A whale!

M: A whale? (Charlie, who is reading nearby, interjects a comment about his own reading, but Marietta continues to focus on James. Then Charlie (C), who has begun to listen, suggests a solution.)

C: A wall. Wall!

M: Ah! That makes sense. That could be a wall, couldn't it? (She speaks to James and points at the illustration.)

J: True.

C: Wall, again. (He leans over and reads the print.)

M: Yes. Let's read the whole sentence together.

M/J/C: He went stick, stick, stick and stood the sunflower up by the wall again.

Initially, James either does not recognize, or can't be bothered to investigate, an unlikely happening. But Marietta asks about the "well," so that James has to acknowledge the problem. He tries other possibilities, but his last suggestion, "whale," makes even less sense. He is having trouble integrating graphophonic and meaning cues. It is Charlie who sees the larger picture and comes up with a reasonable prediction.

Early in the dialogue, James reads, "sticking, sticking, sticking" instead of "stick, stick, stick." We don't worry about a miscue like this. It sounds sensible and perhaps even better than the original text. Later, he reads "You said," but corrects it to "He said." We reinforce such corrections; they indicate that readers are being accountable for meaning.

We don't worry when pupils like Charlie help out. Generally, it is a matter of one pupil at risk assisting another. We acknowledge such contributions, but keep our focus on the original readers. We expect them to take over and make the corrections their own. They are accountable for their own reading, and ultimately must not rely on others.

Communicating Meaning

Writers must consider their readers' needs. Help them by listening to their compositions and, if there's something you don't understand, probe for clarification and explanation. Expect them to express their ideas orally at first. Then, as they are able, encourage them to elaborate in writing.

Nathan (N) draws a child and pastes two small pieces of paper on either side, so they look and act like doors. Writing accompanies his drawing, and he reads it to Lee (L).

N: (Reading:) My sister said, "Let's play hide. I said O.K."
L: Oh! So who is this? Is this you? (She points to the child in the illustration.)
N: (He nods yes.)
L: And is your sister hiding behind there? (She points to one of the "doors.")
N: Yeah.
L: Do you find her?
N: Yeah.
L: Do you? But what room is there, behind that door?
N: It's the.... We hide in the door and we hide in the closet.
L: Oh! It's the door to the closet. You go inside the closet.
N: And I hide there and she didn't find me.
L: She didn't? Where were you then?
N: Under something.

L: Oh! Nathan, you've got a whole story there. I have to go now, but I'd like to hear more about that. Do you think you could write it?

Nathan is an ESL pupil. His initial message is cryptic but, as Lee assumes, he has much more in mind. In a series of responses to her probes, he gradually reveals his story. Now he has the motivation and structure to extend his writing. Lee leaves him with a challenge and Nathan rises to meet it. He describes several more events. The result is a narrative-like piece in which he outwits his sister at a game of hide and seek.

Expect pupils to explain their ideas and their strategies. Ask, "Why do you think...?" and "How did you know to do that?" For example, after Jaspreet reads "The Gingerbread Man," Lee says, "Tell me about the fox." Jaspreet responds, "He's smart." Lee agrees with the answer, but she expects Jaspreet to substantiate her claim. She asks, "What makes you say that?"

The "right" answer is seldom enough. In fact, the best questions don't have a correct answer, they probe for thoughts and opinions. We ask real questions and expect responses which reflect personal views and ideas.

We acknowledge and reinforce all thoughts and opinions. We probe for explanations of unexpected answers, and often find high-quality thinking. We receive interesting insights we could never possibly have imagined.

Moving Toward Conventional Form

Once pupils are writing fluently and spelling many words conventionally, we expect them to review their writing and make judgments on its correctness. We might say, "When you are finished writing, circle the parts you need help with." Then we give the correct renditions or coach them to correct their own work. Some pupils may circle items which are correct. Then we acknowledge and applaud their strategies.

Once pupils demonstrate their understanding of a strategy, they are accountable for its use. If they don't use newly-acquired strategies, we probe their understanding and encourage further refinements. Here are three examples:

1. Bernice circles two misspellings. But there are more that Lee thinks she can recognize. Lee says, "Well, so far so good, but I think you can find more words that need circling. Give it a try." Bernice locates and circles five more words, and Lee gives her the spellings.
2. One day Jillian prints "INoU" and reads, "I know you." She seems to recognize the necessary match between printed letters and spoken words, but on the next day she returns to her previous strategy of printing a string of letters unrelated to her message. Lee says, "I like your story about Santa. But where does it say *Santa* in your writing?" She hopes that Jillian will point to or add an *S* or a *C*. If she doesn't, it's an indication that Jillian has not quite reached that level of development.
3. Kevin reads his writing in sentences, although the sentence markers are missing. Lee says, "A reader would have to read your writing like this:" and in one breath, gasping for air, she reads the entire piece. Kevin interrupts with a laugh, "Oh, I know what I have to do! I have to put in the periods."

. . . .

ORGANIZING THE PROGRAM

Classroom teachers have many responsibilities. Without extra assistance, they often can't meet the specific needs of pupils at risk. Therefore, these pupils may be taught in other settings, such as:

— Special or English as a Second Language (ESL) classes which have a limited number of pupils in full-time attendance.
— Learning Assistance, Resource or English Language centers which pupils attend on a part-time basis.
— Learning clinics, offices or other settings which offer extra-sessional classes and tutoring.

The program works in all these settings, in accordance with the principles outlined in the Introduction. The key to success is pupils who accept their responsibilities and carry out routines independently. The pupils choose writing topics and reading material, and then write and read in any way they can. The teachers are free to observe, coach and evaluate pupils individually, according to the priorities. Our objective is a harmonious working environment which nurtures pupils as they develop toward literacy.

Pupil Groupings

TEACHING SMALL GROUPS

There are many advantages to teaching pupils at risk in small groups of three to five members. The arrangement provides opportunities for both social interaction and individual attention. It enables group members to engage in a wide range of literacy activities, such as reading plays, enacting role dramas, writing cooperatively and solving problems. These activities are purposeful, enjoyable and motivating. At times, the enthusiasm of a single pupil sparks an entire group.

When we teach small groups, we work with them to create an atmosphere of mutual acceptance and respect. We encourage members to listen to others and respond to their ideas and experiences. Their self-esteem grows as they teach and learn from each other.

One of our pupils, David, stutters and stumbles as he reads his own selections, but he looks sideways at Sandra's book, and prompts her when she gets stuck. We find he reads better when he isn't the center of attention. We let this situation continue because David is sustaining Sandra's reading and, at the same time, gaining confidence for himself.

Not all sharing is of such mutual benefit. Another pupil, Scott, constantly interrupts his own and others' writing to ask how words are spelled. He is trying to rely on his classmates' abilities rather than working to develop his own. He is also interfering with everyone's concentration. We do not let such interruptions continue. We judge each situation on its own merits, consider the effects and respond appropriately.

We expect pupils to work in harmony with each other. When there is a problem, we reflect on its source. Perhaps there is a critical difference between members in terms of maturity, interests or ability. One member may be too overbearing, while another is too shy for effective participation.

Group work should motivate pupils, enhance experience and validate the communicative nature of literacy. If this isn't happening, we will respond with a new arrangement of pupils or activities. We find that some children require one-to-one tutoring before they can profit from group sessions.

TUTORING INDIVIDUALS PRIVATELY

When we teach pupils on their own, we can offer them our undivided attention and tailor procedures and expectations to fit their personalities and abilities. They, in turn, can read, write and discuss without being inhibited or distracted by others. This situation can work well, but there *are* drawbacks.

Pupils who experience concentrated attention often develop dependencies. They expect others to initiate, maintain and monitor their work, whereas they should be learning to take on those responsibilities. Therefore, we are careful not to hover over them as they work. We encourage and support, but don't correct or direct. We help pupils become self-sustaining learners by keeping them in control even as they are learning.

ASSISTING IN MAINSTREAM CLASSROOMS

Pupils at risk often make good progress in programs outside mainstream classrooms. But on their return, they find it hard to adjust and apply their new learning. They may experience problems with curriculum, routines or their peers. Thus it makes good sense to provide the extra assistance in the mainstream setting.

Before we enter classrooms to assist pupils at risk, we meet with the teachers to discuss our approach to children, literacy activities and literacy learning. We want the classroom teachers to continue to control their classes, but we don't want our pupils singled out from their peers. We'd like a routine in which both of us observe, coach and take responsibility for the progress of all the pupils.

We and our pupils benefit from such a team-teaching situation. There are two (or more) teachers working with the same pupils, so they get the attention they need. At the same time, we can share observations, signs of progress and teaching strategies, as well as learning from each other. However, if our views aren't compatible, then we are better off teaching these pupils in a separate setting.

Setting

WORK AREAS

Arrange the room so that pupils can carry out their responsibilities independently without disturbing anyone else. Make sure there is room for you to circulate freely and observe pupils at work.

Provide seating for small groups of pupils. We prefer round tables, because there is space for elbows at the edge and supplies in the center. Round tables also encourage group discussion. We make sure there is room for us to pull up a chair for coaching or discussions.

Set aside areas for displaying reading books and writing materials, and for storing pupils' file folders or tote trays. Make display and storage areas accessible, so pupils can easily pick up and put away their work.

If possible, arrange to have a carpeted floor area near a chalk board or bulletin board. The area should be large enough for shared and group activities.

Make use of all opportunities to display functional print. Print captions, labels and names on property and materials. Post reference material on bulletin boards and include alphabets, both upper- and lower-case, in print and cursive forms. Have calendars, and print the day's date in a consistent and conspicuous place.

Reserve bulletin board space for pupils' messages, pinning up pupils' work so that others can see it and respond to it; such displays validate and motivate their efforts.

SUPPLIES

Give each new pupil a file folder or tote tray in which to keep current reading material and all writing papers. Folders work best for students who are writing on newsprint and foolscap paper and maintaining their own Pupil Record Forms. Tote trays are more suitable for emergent readers and writers.

READING MATERIALS

Collect a variety of books for readers at all levels of ability and across a variety of interests and genres. Provide familiar books as well as those which will challenge their experience and ability. We try to offer good literature with attractive illustrations, predictable language and straightforward plot lines.

Display books prominently. They may be on shelves, but long, rectangular tables allow better viewing and space to browse. Keep as many as fifty books on hand. If you think your pupils are overwhelmed by the choice, group books

Pupil's Reading Record

Title	Date Started	Conferencing Points/Commitment/Comments
The Turnip	Oct 8	enormous x, retell ✓, lesson x
		good choice
Henny Penny	Oct 9	retell ✓, "Foxes eat animals
		I'd have run away."
Dark Dark Wood	Oct 11	shared reading, repeated.
The Pancake		shared
Big Little	Oct 12	shared
Little Brown House		shared
Dark Dark Wood	Oct 15	read rapidly & independently!
Jack-in-the Box	Oct 17	shared
Jack-in-the Box	Oct 18	box / big box, I / in
		some good correcting! *

Pupil's Writing Record

Title	Date Started	Conferencing Points/Commitment/Comments
Duta	Sept6	(Data from Star Trek)
The Hoted Hse	Sept7	MC. (The Haunted House) How did they die?
BTT Fucher 4	Sep 10	(Back To The Future IV)
BTT Fucher 4	Sep 12	A Time Boat - What a good idea! Sp✓
BTT Fucher 4	Sep 16	
BTT Fucher 4	Sep 17	
Spdce dge	Sep 18	Good introduction 1. discuss S.P. (Story problem) machines break 2. Develop S.P. (published ✓)
M til cige	Sep 24	(Metal Age)
Cloud age	Sep 26	Why were the evil spirits after them?
Food age	Sep 27	
Jungle cige	Sep 29	What a wonderful theory for how animals come to be. This would be a great introduction to a legend.
Mario age	Oct 1	

according to reading level, topic, theme, author or publisher. We vary our selection and groupings often. Our observations of pupils' choices tell us which books are especially interesting, readable and attractive.

WRITING MATERIALS

Keep writing supplies, drawing materials and extra record forms on shelves or tables. Make them accessible, so that pupils can easily collect and return what they need. Provide a number of sharp pencils, a variety of colored pens or crayons, lined newsprint paper (for first draft writing), lined foolscap (for final copies), blank paper, exercise books with half-lined and half-blank pages, pupil record forms, scissors and tape (for cut-and-paste editing), a stapler and other craft materials.

Keeping Records

RECORD FORMS FOR PUPILS

Prepare printed forms so that pupils can record dates, titles, comments and commitments. (Please refer to the samples on pages 69 and 70) Expect them to keep two forms: one for reading and one for writing. Make them responsible for keeping the forms up-to-date. It's convenient if the forms are stapled to the inside cover of the appropriate folders.

Before pupils begin reading, they record the dates and titles of their selections in the appropriate columns. During or following reading, they note ideas, questions or commitments in the *Comments* column. We may also note development, accomplishment or commitments in this column.

The Writing Record is identical. Before pupils write, they record the dates and proposed titles of their compositions. In the third column, they or we note their commitments regarding the pieces under discussion and any ideas for future writing.

Teacher's Conference Record

Date	Name	Title	Conferencing Points/Priority	Completion Date/Code	Future Plan
Nov. 10	Anita	H.B. to me	@ G.Z - ✓		
	Carrisa	1. Superstar	strategy - skipping much to diff. (difficult) - discuss		
		2. Wombat	strategy - making sense (substituting words) too diff. - sent back to choose		
		3. Oscar	good choice ✓ (Thinks Billy is a puppet controlled by Boy.)		
	Adya	Harriet + Wm.	Rt. (Retell) orally ✓		
	Priya	The Knight			
		+ Dragon	(Rt.) orally ✓ diff. with generalizing lesson		
Nov. 14	Professional Day				

RECORD FORMS FOR TEACHERS

Use the Record Form to record successive observations of one pupil or of a group of pupils. In either case, fill in the date, names of pupils, titles of reading selections or writing topics and brief comments for each observation or conference. Comments are usually diagnostic or reminders of accountability. A clipboard will allow you to carry the form and some notepaper as you circulate among pupils. The notepaper is for more lengthy, anecdotal observations. Previous excerpts are from one of Mayling Chow's reading groups.

Scheduling

Schedule young pupils for regular thirty- to forty-minute sessions. They need to meet often—at least three times a week. During sessions, watch for signs of restlessness and change activities accordingly.

Schedule older, more mature students for longer sessions of about one hour. You may have to pay particular attention to their work and study habits, but if they can complete work on their own time and bring it for review and discussion, then they will not need as many sessions.

Group sessions need to be longer than private tutoring sessions. There must be time for group discussions and activities, as well as for individual coaching and conferences.

Pupils' Responsibilities for Routines

Pupils enter the room quietly, pick up their folders or tote trays and carry them to an available seating area. They locate their work-in-progress and continue from where they left off in the previous session.

Marietta guides her pupils into this routine:

> "Three girls enter, go to shelves, and pick up their folders. They ask for Mrs. Hurst and are told she is coming and that they should carry on with what they are supposed to do. They go to a table, put down their folders and chat amongst themselves. They look around the room (at others working)

> and try to engage in conversation with several boys at the next table. Three other boys enter the room, look around, pick up their folders, and settle at an adjacent table. Mrs. H. enters, surveys the room and comments to the children how wonderful it is that they have organized themselves."

Marietta coaches these pupils to assume responsibility for the routine by stating her expectations and, at the same time, reinforcing their successful compliance. Her matter-of-fact approach guides them without confrontational overtones.

Pupils select their own reading material from the display area. They record the date and title on their Reading Record form and begin to read in any way they can. If they find their selections are unsuitable, they return them to the display and make other choices. In the next excerpt from the same source, Tim follows the routine, thereby taking control of his own reading program:

> "A child, who looks about seven, is working alone. He is reading aloud to himself—going quickly through a book—reciting to himself, turning pages quickly. Toward the end he focuses intently on the last page, closes the book, makes a note in his folder, chooses a second book and reads aloud to himself with gestures and movements. He makes another note in his folder and moves to a third book. He follows the text with his finger. He finishes this book, and gets up and crosses to the book table to make another selection. This routine of selecting a book, reading it and recording in his folder continues for at least fifteen minutes without any intervention or external direction."

Tim chooses his own books. He reads and records his reading in preparation for a later conference with a teacher. He solves his own problems without interrupting the activities of others.

Emergent readers follow the same routine, although they may require assistance in recording dates and titles. When they "read," they use the format of the book, illustrations and prior knowledge to create a meaningful text. When they select a book they already know, they may remember enough of the language and wording to attempt a match with the print.

Emergent writers draw a picture and write about it. They write on successive pages in half-lined, half-blank exercise books. They ask for help to date their work, if necessary. When they are finished, they "read" their messages to a teacher who transcribes it on the back pages of their exercise books.

Pupils assemble and maintain their writing supplies. They decide on topics and write their first drafts on lined newsprint. They use every second line so that there is room for additions or alterations. They note dates, titles and comments on their Writing Record Forms.

When students complete compositions they review them, proofreading or editing as their ability and experience permit. They may sign a schedule to indicate their readiness for a conference. As they await their turn, they begin writing on a new topic or switch to a reading activity.

We do not allow pupils to interrupt our conferences with others. If readers get "stuck" on vocabulary, they make sense of what they can and continue reading. If writers encounter problems, they write what they can and leave spaces for corrections or unrealized ideas, receiving help with such problems during their own conference time.

When pupils change activities or finish a session, they file work-in-progress, including books they are reading, into their folders or tote trays. They return the remaining supplies and reading materials to the display areas. As they leave the room, they put away folders or trays in the designated storage areas.

Teachers' Routines

We organize the setting and guide pupils into following the routines. Within this structure, they can operate pretty much on their own. Some pupils may try to take advantage of the freedom. We explain the division of responsibilities by saying, "You're in charge of your reading and writing, but I'm in charge of the room. You can't interrupt or bother other people. Now, what's your plan for today?" Then we help them carry out their intentions.

Our program involves immersing pupils in reading and writing. We organize group sessions for specific purposes and set up routines for independent work. We observe what pupils are doing and how they are doing it. The result is on-going evaluation which is the basis of our coaching.

In the chapters which follow, we set out Reading and Writing Programs and Evaluation in detail. The chapters are separate, but the activities overlap and are even concurrent in the day-to-day operation of the program.

The regular routine involves pupils reading and writing independently. We circulate among them, observe and perhaps nod and murmur our approval. At times, we pause to listen to oral reading or ask about selections. We ask writers to explain their ideas or read what they have written so far. We record our observations and coach according to our priorities.

We stay close to emergent readers and writers, to help them record dates, maintain their strategies and stay focused on their work. We observe and note significant events and transcribe their written messages as read onto the back page of their writing books.

We arrange individual or group conferences in which pupils read and discuss their reading and writing. We encourage them to share and help each other as long as the results are generally beneficial. We keep our routines flexible and seize the teachable moments.

. . . .

THE READING PROGRAM

Immersion in Reading

Many pupils at risk have not had much experience with books or reading. Therefore, our first priority is to immerse them in reading. We choose traditional fairy tales and myths, as well as stories of action and adventure. We include a number of styles and genres, including poems, plays, non-fiction, storybooks and informational materials. We read books chosen by our pupils. We create a comfortable setting for reading and invite pupils to listen and enjoy.

Here is a routine you can use to introduce a new selection. Begin by reading the title and showing the cover illustration. Suggest pupils predict the subject, character, mood or plot. Find out what pupils know about the topic, and provide any information they will need to understand the reading.

A pupil chooses a non-fiction book with a picture of a juicy hamburger on the cover. He wants Lee (L) to read it to his group. This group has pupils (P)—one of whom is a girl named Danielle (D)—from different cultural and language backgrounds, so Lee helps them to investigate the topic before reading.

L: Have you ever eaten a hamburger?
P: Yes! Yes! Yes! (They all respond, except for Danielle.)
D: No!
L: Really? Well, what can we tell Danielle about hamburgers?
P: You buy them.
P: My mom makes them.
P: Like at McDonald's. (Amidst this chorus of suggestions, Danielle contributes an idea.)
D: They have meat. It's like a sandwich.

L: I thought you'd never had a hamburger!
D: But I have seen one (laughing).
L: Now I want you to tell me all the different things you might put into a hamburger.

Suggestions pour out, but they can't come up with the English names of several items. Lee asks for appearance, use, taste—all the describing words she can think of. When she is sure they have thoroughly searched their memories for information and experience, she provides the missing vocabulary.

At times you may wish to record what pupils know or predict about a topic before you read. Then, afterwards, you can encourage them to reconsider their ideas and add new information. But don't prolong the preparation. A successful introduction arouses pupils' interest and makes them eager for the reading to begin.

We start reading when the moment feels right, and we read with enthusiasm and emotion, so that pupils experience the power of the selection. Sometimes we focus on the illustrations; at other times on the setting, plot, characters or other information in the text. We vary the focus according to the demands of the text and the abilities of our pupils.

When we read to pupils, we expect them to follow and make sense of the text, and we encourage their responses. For example, when Lee reads about a kind daughter and a mean sister, Saspreet exclaims, "Oh, it's just like Cinderella!" When Lee reads about a witch who forgets where she puts things, Mark giggles on every page, saying, "She won't know where it is, but I do!" Such comments let Lee know that pupils are paying attention and incorporating the experience into their learning.

As a story unfolds, you can ask pupils to revise their predictions. Ask what they are wondering about, and what information they want or need to know. At times, you may wish to pause and summarize the plot or information. Manage such interruptions so that they enhance pupils' understanding without spoiling the effect. Keep up the pace!

After reading a fictional selection, ask pupils to retell the story, identify story problems and attempted solutions, or consider the lesson. Encourage them to connect the reading with their own life experience. Some pupils will respond easily, but others will have trouble expressing themselves and be reluctant to air their views. We model appropriate responses, help them take turns and build on the answers of others.

Pupils may be restless and unable to concentrate for any length of time. In this case, we bring the reading to a close, place a bookmark between the appropriate pages and promise to continue another day.

SHIFTING RESPONSIBILITY

Pupils need activities that move them easily from shared to independent reading. We invite groups to join us in reading a "Big Book," a chart, or the enlarged print of a reading selection on an overhead projector. Once they seem comfortable and confident in this choral reading situation, we shift the responsibility to individuals. We ask for volunteers to read certain lines by themselves or together with friends. Selections which have repeated phrases or refrains are particularly useful for such activities.

We set up situations in which pupils share the responsibility for reading. They may read refrains or alternate sentences, paragraphs or pages. This is an occasion of reading together to enjoy books and stories and is definitely not a performance. We make sure it is an enjoyable experience by observing their responses for confidence and strengths.

Lee sits at a round table with a small group of reluctant readers aged ten or eleven. She begins the first session by asking what kind of books they like to read. At first, they say they have no interest in reading. But then they search her collection and find several well-illustrated books of fairy tales and myths they think they might enjoy. The stories have clear plot lines and are relatively short, yet the presentation is appropriate for their age level.

Lee chooses one and involves her pupils in predicting its contents. She places the book flat on the table where they can see it, and begins reading. As she reads, she encourages pupils to comment on the story or illustrations. After several sessions, one pupil asks to read, so Lee begins a routine in which she reads one sentence and passes the book to the pupil on her right. He reads the next sentence and passes the book to his right. Soon all the pupils are reading in turn as the book moves around the table.

Lee observes her pupils and finds they are following the text and asking questions when something doesn't make sense. They notice the sentence breaks and are ready when it's their turn to read.

We suggest you follow the lead of pupils' interest and attention. Elicit facts and opinions. Reinforce all efforts to think and consider. If readers look to you for help, refer their problems to the rest of the group, then encourage group members to make suggestions and try out alternatives. In this way, they practise problem-solving strategies and learn from each other. Reading becomes a cooperative project.

Some stories have a number of characters who speak in direct quotations. You can add interest and realism by assigning roles to pupils and having them read the spoken words of their characters. If you read the difficult bits of description and narration yourself, you will keep pupils on their toes watching for punctuation and listening for their cues.

Read plays together. Then, after several group readings, have pupils take on individual roles. You can ask them to draw and cut out likenesses of their characters. They can make puppets by attaching them to sticks or old rulers with glue. Pupils at risk often read more freely when the attention shifts from them to their puppets. Once they are confident with their roles, they may enjoy presenting an informal puppet play to selected guests, friendly classmates or younger pupils.

We use the same activities when we teach individuals in tutorial sessions. We act as if we are partners engaged in an enjoyable activity, rather than prompters who correct words and text. We proceed at a reasonable pace and don't make individual turns too long. We want to shift the responsibility for reading to our pupils, but we don't want to generate anxiety or lose their attention.

MOVING TOWARD CONVENTIONAL READING

Emergent readers need help to integrate graphophonic strategies into their repertoire. Begin by finding out what they already know about print. You can print letters of the alphabet in upper- and lower-case forms and ask for their names. Upper-case letters are the most distinctive, so don't be surprised if children identify them first. If they have difficulty remembering letters, create memory cues, such as making the letter *S* into a snake.

Find out what commonly-used words pupils recognize. Include their names and those of family, friends and classmates. In order to discover the strategies that work for them, ask how they recognize and remember such words. Print identified words on cards so that pupils can begin a collection of words they recognize at sight. We call this their *word bank*.

Enlarge their word bank by taking a walk along a hallway of the school or along a street in their neighborhood and asking them to find words they know. Pause at printed signs or messages and ask what they mean, what the words say and how they know what they say.

With help, children will be able to use context to identify such signs as *GIRLS*, *BOYS*, *OFFICE*, *STOP* and *McDonald's*. Copy the identified words on a sheet of notepaper as they watch. Encourage them to identify the letters as you print them and to notice their sequence. Identify and print about six words on a first walk.

At a later time, show pupils the notepaper and see if they can read the words. Transfer the words they identify onto cards, and add them to their word bank. If they don't recognize the words, take them back to the original source and ask again. Repeat the sequence of identifying and adding new words several times, or for as long as pupils stay interested and motivated.

Immerse the pupils in activities which involve reading and following signs and messages. Show them how they can use their word cards to create messages that others can follow. Adapt your procedures to meet pupils' understanding.

Here is another way of using the words in pupils' word banks to extend their vocabulary. Print a word (for example, *boys*), then change the first letter to form the new word (*toys*). Many pupils enjoy making lists of such rhyming words and arranging them into word families, but rhyming words are not always spelled the same. Be prepared to recognize and discuss exceptions.

Note significant development on the Record Form for Teachers or in anecdotal form. Regularly collect and analyze samples of each pupil's independent writing and reading. In a positive and encouraging atmosphere, pupils will show what they can do and alert you to their needs.

Reading Independently

COACHING STRATEGIES TO SELECT READING

We coach strategies for choosing suitable reading material. We say, "We have lots of books here. Take your time, look through them and find one to read." We observe their approach (confident or hesitant) and their search (careful or hasty). You may think that pupils at risk cannot make appropriate selections, but they can if you give the right help at the right time. Let them know that learning proceeds by trial and error.

How do readers make appropriate choices? They ask themselves many questions. Is the subject interesting? Can they make sense of it? What will they learn? Do they wish to read for information or entertainment; silently or aloud; carefully or rapidly? Do they intend to devour the plot, savor the language or skim for information?

Once pupils select their books, suggest they open them and read a page or two. Don't hurry them or make suggestions of your own. Go along with their choices, even if you think the text is uninteresting or too difficult. You may be surprised at the suitability! In any case, pupils gain expertise and confidence when they discover their own errors.

Coaching pupils to choose suitable material is a key priority. In this example, Lee (L) approaches Jimmy (J) who has quickly selected a book with a number of animals depicted on a colorful cover. He is taking it to his seat.

L: Oh! You've chosen a book about animals. Can you tell me about them? (She points to the cover illustration.)

J: Yeah! This one's a tiger. It lives in the jungle.... (He reveals a great deal of information and interest without any hesitation.)

L: Good for you! You know a lot. How about opening the book and reading a bit aloud.

J: Okay. (He reads a few words, but soon comes to a complete stop.)

J: I don't know the words. (He looks to Lee for assistance.)
L: And what does that tell you?
J: It's too hard.
L: Good for you! You realize that. Well, it seems to be an interesting book. Would you like me to read it to the group later?
J: (He nods.)
L: Good; I'll put it on my desk. Now, what can you do about your own reading?
J: Get another book?
L: That's the idea. What could you do differently this time?
J: Try some of the pages?
L: Good thinking!

Lee's initial response confirms and reinforces the suitability of Jimmy's choice in terms of his interests and knowledge. Then she helps him judge its appropriateness for independent reading. When he discovers that he has a problem, she makes sure he has a strategy for its solution.

Once pupils have made a successful choice, help them reflect on their strategies. Say, "What made you decide to choose this book? What did you like about it? Was it too easy, too difficult or just right?" Confirm indications of a thoughtful approach.

Some pupils like to read old favorites again and again. Others choose to read very easy selections. We generally accept such choices. Each reading provides opportunities for pupils to build much-needed confidence, to consolidate previous learning and to integrate the strategies of fluent readers.

COACHING STRATEGIES DURING READING

Readers need feedback on their use of strategies. Therefore, we pause beside them, listen to their oral reading and comment according to our priorities. Often, we just murmur, "Uh huh," "Yes," Hmmm," or "Interesting!" These are signs we can voice without interrupting a reading, and they let pupils know of our interest and approval.

If readers pause or ask for help, don't be too quick to respond. Encourage them to find ways to solve their own problems. In the dialogue that follows, Marietta works to connect with Vicki's ideas, confirm what she is doing right and extend her thinking. These coaching strategies are interrelated and reinforce each other.

Vicki (V) is seven years old and learning to read in English, her second language. She selects June Melser's version of *Little Red Hen* to read. Marietta (M) listens and coaches Vicki's strategies:

M: *Little Red Hen*. What a good choice! I think I saw you reading a different version of that story last week.
V: (Nods and smiles.)
M: You're comfortable? Then let's begin.
V: Little red hen lived with a cat, and a rat, and a, mm-mouse. Little red hen said, ummm..."I will make a cake."
M: Uh-huh....
V: "Who will get me some cookies" no... "eggs for the cake?"
M: Yes, that couldn't say *cookies*, could it? She needs eggs.
V: "I want," said the cat.
M: Hmmm?
V: "I want," said the rat. "I want," said the mouse.
M: Hmmm?
V: "Then I will get them...myself..."
M: Good thinking!
V: ...said little red hen. So she did.
M: Can you tell me what happened there, in your own words?
V: Ummm...that she maked that herself.
M: Why?
V: Because everybody wanted it—the cat and the rat and the mouse.
M: Ah! But what did she ask?
V: Who will get me some eggs for the cake? I want...
M: Does that make sense? What could we do there?
V: They have to get.... No, they have to get some things. Then she will make it.
M: Oh. And what are they saying?
V: They saying they want different things.

M: Hmmm. Let's see if that makes sense.... Well, don't let yourself get stuck. Keep on reading and think about it.

V: Little red hen said, "Who will get me some flour for the...cake?" "I what?" No, ..."I want," said the cat.

M: Would the cat say that? Does that make sense? What else could that be besides *want*?

V: Won't! (Obviously thrilled.)

M: From the sound of your voice, I can tell you're sure that's right. What a good idea!

V: "I won't," said the rat. "I won't," said the mouse. "Then I will get myself," said the red hen. So she did. (Vicki looks at Marietta and says, "She will get herself!")

M: Ah, I see. Let's keep going.

V: Little red hen said, "Who will get me some, some...milk for the cake?"

M: Hmmm. How did you know?

V: I sound it...*M-A-L-K—milk*!

M: Good idea, but I saw your eyes going down here, too. You were using a good idea from there—from the picture. Good for you!

V: "I won't," said the cat. "I won't," said the rat. "I won't," said the mouse. "Then I will get myself," said the red hen. And she, no.... So she did. Little red...little red hen said, "Who will help me make the cake?" "I won't," said the cat. "I won't," said the rat. "I won't," said the mouse. "Then I will do it," no.... "Then I will...make, mmm—it?" No. "Then I will make it myself,"

M: Good correcting!

V: ...said little red hen. So she did. "And who will hep...help me eat the cake?" said the little red hen...said little red hen. "I will," said the cat. "I will," said the rat. "I will," said the mouse. "No, you will not," said little red hen. "You will not, help, me eat, it." "I will eat it by myself...eat it myself."

M: Oh, good correcting.

V: So, she did.

M: Yes, she did eat it. And that's the end of the story.

We connect with pupils when we acknowledge their experience, knowledge and understanding. At the beginning of the session, Marietta builds a bridge to Vicki's experience with another version of *Little Red Hen*. Throughout, Marietta responds positively to the reading. Her comments show that she is following the plot and, at the same time, they acknowledge Vicki's reading competence.

We confirm successful strategies by drawing attention to them. Thus we make those that are intuitive or implicit become explicit and under the reader's control. Marietta is both confirming Vicki's correction and identifying an effective strategy when she says, "...I saw your eyes going down here, too. You were using a good idea from there—from the picture. Good for you." Later, she confirms Vicki's ability to make her own decisions and judge her own success by saying, "From the sound of your voice, I can tell you're sure that's right."

We extend readers' knowledge and strategies when we clarify and redirect their thinking. At first Marietta doesn't respond when Vicki reads "I want" for "I won't". She hopes Vicki will realize that the reading doesn't make sense or sound quite right, and initiate her own correction. When Vicki persists with the reading, Marietta asks for a summary and Vicki responds, "Everybody wanted it—the cat, the rat and the mouse." and "They saying they want different things."

Vicki has manipulated the story to fit with her reading, but she has misinterpreted the story. Marietta suggests Vicki "think about that." Vicki tries another solution and Marietta asks, "What else could that be besides *want*?" Now Vicki responds "won't" and immediately knows she is right. With Marietta's help, Vicki has extended her thinking.

We help pupils like Vicki to think their way through their problems. The next time they get stuck, they will draw on the strategies and confidence they have gained from the experience.

COACHING WHICH FOLLOWS READING

At times, we interrupt silent readers and ask about their reading. We say, "What have you learned so far?" or "Tell me about what you are reading." In mid-story we ask, "What do you think will happen next?" Such questions do much more than monitor pupils' comprehension. They ask pupils to use past events to predict future possibilities and emphasize the purposeful, predictive nature of reading.

Some pupils have difficulty recalling events and stating ideas. We support them by:

— Asking them to retell short episodes rather than whole stories.
— Providing structure for organizing events and ideas.
— Rephrasing or summarizing their ideas before asking them to continue.

When we published *Whole Language: Practical Ideas*, in 1991, we suggested you probe deeply for pupils' understanding of the characters, plot and main ideas of a story, asking them about the problems in the plot, the attempts to solve them, the lessons and the story's relevance to their lives.

After Vicki (V) reads *Little Red Hen*, Marietta (M) initiates a conference about the story. She begins by asking Vicki to tell the story in her own words. Vicki is confused, but is it the task or the story? Notice how Marietta's comments and questions clarify the matter and enable Vicki to complete the retelling:

M: Oh, I see you really enjoyed that story. Good reading! Now tell me about the story—in your own words.
V: The ca-, the mou-, the little red hen gonna make a cake. And the cat said who-, the little red hen said, "Who will help me to get...the...um, um....
M: What did she want?
V: A cake.
M: And then what happened?
V: Then the little red hen make it. Then they all finished make the cake. And they eat it, all of them.
M: They eat it, all of them? Is that the way it was in the book?
V: I use it myself.
M: Oh, you're making your own story! But what did the story talk about?
V: That, um; help me.
M: Yes?

V: And they didn't.
M: They didn't?
V: Yeah, but the cake, to eat it, they didn't. But they didn't because the red, little red hen said, "No," because they didn't help her, see? And that's not fair. Because they didn't help her. And that's why.
M: That's why what?
V: That's why they did, can't eat the cake.
M: Yes, that was the trouble, wasn't it? The other animals wouldn't help the little red hen. Has something like that ever happened to you?
V: No.
M: No? Why not?
V: Because I help my mother.
M: Do you? And so you get to share all the things that your family has? Isn't that nice. You don't even need to learn that lesson. You already know it.
V: Yeah!
M: Good thinking!
V: And I know how to cook!
M: Great!

Vicki begins by trying to repeat the exact words of the story. Then she tries to create her own version of the story. Marietta frames two key questions to clear up the confusion. She asks, "What did she want?" and "What happened next?" Such questions provide structure for the retelling without adding any new information.

The questions enable Vicki to start again. And this time she gets to the heart of the matter. Marietta helps again by restating the main point, "Yes, that was the trouble...." The paraphrase not only reinforces Vicki's understanding, it is also a model for oral expression. Like many pupils, Vicki needs help with oral as well as written language. When Vicki responds, "I help my mother." she clearly indicates her understanding.

Readers like to retell because it gives them a chance to say what is important to them. As well as retelling stories, they can retell what they have learned from reading non-fiction. In this case, they find out what they can remember and understand from their reading, and they notice what they have missed. Students discover that retelling is an aid to independent learning.

A retelling lets us know what readers are getting out of their reading. We find out what they remember and how they organize and relate ideas. More importantly, it gives us a route into their thinking. Notice in the previous example how Marietta extends Vicki's retelling to reach a deeper level of meaning. Retellings work for pupils and teachers. They lead to working relationships built on mutual trust and confidence.

. . . .

THE WRITING PROGRAM

Immersion in Writing

When we write, we invite pupils to observe and participate. We let them see what we are doing and hear what we are thinking. We voice our ideas and strategies, because the more they observe writers in action the more they will learn what writing involves and how to engage in it.

We invite children to read along as we write messages on charts or chalk boards. An example is this message that Mayling Chow writes to her pupils who are learning English as a Second Language (ESL).

> Good morning, people.
> Today is June the 20th.
> It's almost time for us to
> begin our summer holidays. I
> wonder what we will do.
> Will we go to camp? Will
> we visit our relatives?
> Will some of us move
> to another neighborhood?
> Maybe some lucky person will
> go to Disneyland. Well, good luck
> in whatever you do.

Such personal messages attract and hold pupils' attention. They enable them to experience writing in progress and thus understand more about the writing process. They also provide practice in reading.

We explore different kinds of writing, such as directions, reports, plans, invitations, letters, stories or notes. With more mature students, we discuss styles and genres. As we write, we talk about drafts, proofreading, carets, editing, revision and other writing conventions.

We engage in discussions about possible topics for writing. We ask children to recall experiences, retell favorite stories and build new stories on the ideas of others. We list the topics chosen by favorite authors. We compare different versions of favorite stories, such as *Little Red Hen*. These are opportunities to stimulate thinking, motivate writing and practise oral composition.

SHIFTING RESPONSIBILITY

Our first priority is to enable pupils to engage in and to enjoy meaningful writing. Here is a procedure for shifting the responsibility for composition. Begin with the subject and the purpose for a piece of writing, asking children to suggest what to write about and how to begin. You might list their ideas first. Then they take turns at dictation while you write their words on chart paper or a chalk board.

As you write, emphasize connections between the words in speech and in print. Reread phrases, sentences or the whole piece. Ask if it makes sense and sounds right. Encourage pupils to suggest improvements, and handle their suggestions as revisions or additions.

Once children are comfortable composing written language, shift some more responsibility. Let them help with the transcription. As you write, hesitate at appropriate points and ask for help with spelling, punctuation or wording. Be sure to keep the importance of these surface features in perspective—the focus is the communicative needs of readers.

Initiate an exchange of short notes or informal letters. We reserve a small area of bulletin board for pinned messages and set up a class mailbox. We write notes to pupils and pin them on the "message board" or post them in the mailbox. We encourage them to write back and to correspond with others. A flourishing correspondence helps create a writing community.

All pupils at risk need help when they are required to organize and write reports based on reading or research. Here is a procedure for initiating report writing. Identify a topic. It may arise from previous discussions or another area of the students' curriculum. Print it on the chalk or bulletin board, and draw a circle around it, like a sun. Ask students what they know about the topic and record their information as a radiating schema around the "sun." Ask them what they might find out about the topic. Record these ideas and have each pupil choose one or two to investigate.

Ask pupils how they will find the answers to their questions. They might suggest strategies such as going to the library for books, interviewing knowledgable people or observing events. Everyone needs a specific idea of how to proceed. Then they can disperse to follow up on their ideas.

When the group reassembles, have pupils review and re-value the schema. They insert new ideas and then categorize and label the information. Then they use it to write individual or group reports. Children need to repeat this experience a number of times before they can undertake self-directed projects.

We gradually shift the responsibility for writing to pupils, so that they become more and more involved but without being overwhelmed by details. Even reluctant writers will find they can participate. If their attention span is short, we keep the sessions short. We want them to *enjoy* the writing process.

MOVING TOWARD CONVENTIONAL WRITING

Emergent writers ascribe meaning to writing representations that are not readable by others. Expect them to draw a picture, and then write about it in any way they can. As they work, note their strategies and keep track of their intentions.

Emiliano is an emergent writer. Although he has attended school for three years, he hasn't made much headway learning to write or read. He is learning in his second language, and his speech is difficult to understand, but Lee observes and suspects that he knows more than his work indicates:

"9:15 Emiliano is wandering around the room, not writing. Lee, who is listening to someone else read, seats him at an adjacent table. He leans over and says, "I don't have a story." Lee tells him it is his job to come up with one. He turns around and starts to write.

9:30 Lee turns around to Emiliano and asks him to read his writing. He reads, "Autobot is bigger than Megatron." Lee asks if he can draw a picture to show that comparison. He shows some resistance, and she turns to another pupil.

9:35 Lee returns to Emiliano, who has still not drawn a picture. She rereads his sentence and stays with him, her body language indicating interest. He draws two figures. One is much smaller, has an *E* on his shirt, and radiates strength—he is obviously the winner. Lee asks him how Megatron could win if he is so small. Emiliano very excitedly launches into an explanation of Megatron's special powers. Lee acknowledges his explanation by saying, "It gives me pictures in my mind."

Emergent writers use drawings and representations of writing to record, and then they "read" their messages. We accept scribble and letter-like symbols, but if they only draw and don't attempt writing in any form, we use the content to probe for ideas and extensions. Try to comment or phrase questions so that children extend their ideas orally. Useful starters are:

— Tell me more about....
— I see a person here in your drawing. Who is it? What's happening?
— You and your sister are playing, and I see a sun in your drawing. When did this happen?

To encourage emergent writers to use letter-sound connections in writing, ask them to point to their representations as they read. In this way you'll discover whether they follow the left-to-right and the top-to-bottom conventions of written English. You will also see whether they are matching sounds and letters. For example, Mandy prints *S-P-M-E-K* and reads "Superman is good." She uses a single letter to represent the first sound of each syllable or word. The *E* is for /i/ and the *K* is for /g/, a letter-name strategy.

We take care to acknowledge all such strategies. For example, after Barry "reads" a message about the sun, Lee responds, "I see an *s* here on your page. *S* for *ssssun*. Good for you! How did you know to do that?" Her response confirms and reinforces his strategy. It also asks him to reflect on his understanding. Such thinking will accelerate his progress towards the conventional.

We expect emergent writers to clarify and elaborate their ideas orally at first. However, at any sign of interest, we encourage them to add to their drawing or writing. Additions and changes are a sign of progress. We record the date, message and significant events and strategies in the back of their writing books.

Writing Independently

GETTING STARTED

We expect pupils to select their own writing supplies, sit down, decide on their topics and start writing. They record the date and their proposed titles on their Writing Record forms. For first drafts, they use lined newsprint and write on every second line so that there is space for later improvements and additions.

Pupils at risk are often reluctant to begin. They have experienced writing as an exercise they do "for a teacher" and in order to practise the "skills" of spelling, grammar and punctuation. We counteract such attitudes with clear expectations for *meaning*, such as "I am interested in what you have to say. Don't worry about spelling or handwriting. This is a first draft." Then we let them proceed on their own.

We keep an eye on all our writers, and when they seem uncertain, we offer interest and encouragement. Sometimes we remark on the topic or title, saying "Oh! You've got a good idea there! That *will* be interesting." Sometimes we read their first few sentences, then respond to the meaning and wonder, "What will happen next?"

More confident pupils read their own writing, and we respond to their meaning. Sometimes they discover they are not interested in developing particular topics. Then we encourage them to make other choices. We discuss, but we don't let talking become a substitute for writing. We say, "You've an interesting idea, there. Write it down. I'll be back soon to find out what you have to say."

Pupils often write more easily when they are not the center of attention, so we support writers with our presence, but we don't intrude. We may sit beside or among them and become engrossed in writing of our own. In this way, we're also modeling appropriate writing behavior. Later on, everyone, including ourselves, shares their writing. This activity suggests we are a community of writers.

COACHING STRATEGIES DURING WRITING

Help pupils to improve their writing at the most productive time—while they are actually doing it. Gently interrupt and ask them to read or tell about their topic. If they notice omissions, ambiguities, redundancies or awkwardness of expression, expect them to make changes then and there. Follow their lead to help them find and restructure problem areas.

Investigate pupils' hesitations with questions like "I noticed that you stopped for a moment. Were you thinking about something?" If they offer an oral elaboration or correction, say "Yes, that *is* important. Can you write that in now? Show me where it would go." Offer support and, if appropriate, demonstrate the use of editorial markings.

Carlos (C) is writing when Marietta (M) approaches him for a conference. Notice how she confirms and extends his thinking. The discussion gives him confidence and motivates further writing.

M: Are you starting a new story?
C: (He nods.)
M: What kind of a story?
C: *Cosmic Cow.*
M: What an interesting title! It makes me see pictures in my mind. What does Cosmic Cow look like?
C: She is a girl, and she's big and fat and has a cape and flies.
M: Are there any other characters in your story?
C: There's a boy...and he can't do his work...and Cosmic Cow helps him—but it doesn't say that in the story.
M: Hmmm! Are you going to put that in your story?
C: Yes!

And Carlos begins to write.

When writers talk about their topics, they speak naturally and often include extra details. If you ask the right question at the right time, you may unleash a flood of ideas. Encourage them to put these ideas into writing, but don't feed them your ideas. Expect children to maintain control of their own writing.

When we notice inconsistencies between children's writing and their intentions, we ask about them. We have found that some pupils don't edit because they don't want "to mess up" their paper. We remind them that these are their first drafts, and they may have to "make them messy" in order to make their meaning clear.

FOCUSING ON CONTENT AFTER WRITING

Individual conferences form a major part of our daily routine. We expect writers to prepare for these conferences by rereading their writing and improving it as they can. If they have finished their pieces and are waiting for a conference, we expect them to begin new topics.

At a conference, writers read their writing aloud. We function as an audience which listens and tries to understand their intentions. This is not always an easy task. We check our perceptions by asking questions, paraphrasing ideas, requesting drawings, or offering related experiences of our own.

During a conference, we confine our questions to one aspect of a pupil's work. Pupils find it easiest to add on at the end of a piece, cross out duplications and insert words or phrases, so we suggest these revisions first. If they resist changing their writing, we accept oral explanations and drawings. It takes many successful writing experiences before pupils at risk become fluent and flexible writers.

In addition, we hold group conferences, which are much like the reading conferences that have already been described. We invite a writer to read a piece aloud. The other members become the audience by listening and responding with questions, comments and appreciation. We expect group members to respond in a serious manner. Then writers will be motivated to read and discuss their ideas. They're also keen to begin their next piece of writing. They feel good about writing and about themselves as writers.

Pupils may stop writing to ask for certain spellings. Explain the interrupting effect of such requests and do not provide spellings. Suggest they manage as well as they can and circle the problem words. Help the pupils out with these words only after they have finished writing. At that time, you may wish to draw attention to certain conventions or strategies for spelling.

Encourage capable spellers to proofread for errors. You might say, "Some of your words are hard to read. I'd like you to find some of these words and circle them. Then I'll help you with the spelling." Expect them to find at least three. Provide the spellings of the identified words and ignore the rest. At times we ask, "How do you know that these words are a problem?" If possible, we use their responses to extend their strategies.

Some pupils seem at risk because of their slow progress in spelling, but we resist the temptation to focus on it alone. We immerse them in writing and encourage them to spell in any way they can. Then we observe their strategies. Sometimes spelling is not the main problem. And, in any case, pupils who write frequently generally improve their spelling.

Sharon doesn't have workable spelling strategies so finds writing frustrating and difficult.

Lee uses several strategies to help Sharon to write and spell. First, she scribes as Sharon composes orally. She wants Sharon to develop composition strategies without being overwhelmed by her difficulties with transcription.

Second, she works directly with transcription. She has Sharon list all the words she can spell. Then Lee asks Sharon how she learned these words. It seems that she remembers the look of words, so Lee suggests Sharon choose one word to memorize every day. This activity increases her list of known words immensely. Lee monitors Sharon's progress by dictating the listed words in sentences. The words she misspells are either taken off the list or relearned—it's Sharon's choice.

Two additional strategies increase Sharon's resources. She learns to add prefixes and suffixes to the words on her list and thereby creates new vocabulary. She also begins to skim texts to find and copy the vocabulary she needs. With these strategies, she can begin to write independently.

Adapt your coaching to meet individual needs. Observe pupils' strengths and try techniques which build on those strengths. Evaluate the results and readjust techniques as needed, but take care that pupils continue to realize the communicative purpose of their writing.

Some pupils read their writing with intonation and inflection, yet they haven't marked the punctuation. We read it back to them, and our breathless and monotonous reading usually nudges them to recognize the problem. We ask what they can do about it. If they aren't sure, we often suggest they consult a book and discover how published authors handle the problem.

In this dialogue, Marietta (M) explores Carlos' (C) understanding of the convention of quotation marks. She doesn't prescribe the convention, but draws him into seeing what it could add to his text:

M: There are other things I want to ask you about... you've put some little drawings in; you haven't read them. Can you tell me about them? Should they be read by a reader?

C: (Mumble.)

M: That's the cow saying that? Is there a way we can put that in the story? (She points to a particular place in his writing.)

C: I don't know.

M: I wonder how books do that. Let's pretend someone wants to say something to someone.

C: It says "they said."

M: Yes. Can you put that in?

Carlos begins inserting quotations marks and the necessary text. He goes on to find other places in the story where there is talking. He rereads the ending and looks up, smiling. At the end of the conference, Marietta compliments him on how much he has shown the reader.

Marietta's coaching is particularly powerful because Carlos feels the solution is his own discovery. If he omits the convention in future pieces, Marietta can say, "Carlos, remember the Cosmic Cow story? Remember how you added quotation marks? Can you do that again in this story? That will make it easier to read." Chances are he will be ready and able to comply.

We note such information on our record forms and the pupils do the same on theirs. We build our coaching on pupils' knowledge and understanding. When we succeed in drawing out insights, we expect pupils to incorporate them into future work. We make and hold them accountable for that aspect of the writing process.

PUBLICATION

Encourage reasonably fluent writers to select one of their drafts to prepare for publication. At the first conference, consider aspects of content and composition. Choose one point for pupils to revise. When they have attended to it, suggest proofreading. Aim for self-discovery and self-correction at all times. Do not worry about the errors which remain. Once pupils publish a piece of writing, make it available to other readers.

Pupils need time—lots of time—to write for their own purposes in their own way. In the regular classroom, this time is seldom available, least of all for pupils at risk. We give them this time. We don't try to hurry progress by insisting they work on a piece until it is conventionally correct.

At times, our pupils spend an entire session writing independently. We do not interrupt, as we are delighted that this can happen. Children immersed in writing are teaching themselves. When we become superfluous, we know they are no longer at risk.

. . . .

EVALUATION

Evaluation is an exciting adventure of observations, analyses and insights. We observe pupils' attitudes, their strategies and their completed work. Every detail may be significant. Small signs of progress encourage us as well as our pupils, by letting us know that our coaching is on the right track. Lack of progress suggests we reassess our approach. When we evaluate pupils we are also evaluating the effectiveness of our program.

Evaluating Learning

We note our observations on Teachers' Record forms during and after events, and we file longer anecdotes with the forms. These records help us establish baseline data and recognize changes in strategies, understanding and attitude. From time to time, we review our records and reflect on a pupil's development. Sometimes we discover significant features not obvious at the time of recording.

We encourage pupils to notice their own progress. They review their own Record forms to note the number of books they have read and the compositions they have written. They listen to audiotapes of their reading to identify developing strategies. They reread previous compositions to discover changes in approach and perception. Their self-esteem soars as they recognize their progress.

In this section, we describe three aspects of evaluation, but the aspects are not distinct—they overlap and influence each other. Improvement in one category usually leads to improvement in all categories. Such change creates opportunities for a fresh approach to demonstrations, group activities and coaching. The following routines and questions are a guide to making accurate and useful evaluations.

During demonstrations and group activities, consider questions such as the ones which follow:

- Do pupils watch and listen attentively?
- Do they try to participate and offer ideas?
- Do their contributions relate to the topic at hand and are they predictable or interesting and original?
- Do they enjoy listening to a reading?
- Can they follow and understand the text?
- When engaged in group writing, do they predict, offer ideas and suggest appropriate wording?

Observe their responses to others in the group:

- Do they listen, take turns and build on ideas?
- Do they offer differing interpretations in a positive way?
- Do they try to cooperate and consider others' feelings?
- Are they good-natured, open and positive in their approach?

Other important factors to consider include:

- How do they carry out the established routine?
- Do they choose suitable reading material?
- Do they begin writing without asking for help with topic selection?
- Do they work independently?
- Do they seem motivated to read and to write?
- Are they calm and controlled or fidgety and constantly moving around?
- Do they stay with a task until it is done?

Observe pupils' responses to your coaching:

- Do they pay attention and respond appropriately to comments and questions?
- Are they willing to read aloud, summarize a storyline and make predictions?
- Are they willing to read, explain and clarify their writing?
- Do they spontaneously self-correct, once they realize an error?

Observe pupils as they choose materials:

- Do they look through the books carefully?
- Do they open and read a portion of the text?
- Do they pay attention to the names of the author, the illustrator and the series?
- Do they choose books they have already read, new books by familiar authors, or books read during demonstrations and group activities?
- Do they reflect on their strategies for choosing and their choices?
- Do they read their choices through to completion?

Establish regular intervals for recording pupils' reading on audiotape. In the case of document miscues, fill in a Miscue Record and analyze their use of the cue systems. Record their retelling. Discover and analyze what pupils retain and comprehend after reading.

Observe pupils as they begin writing:

- How do they select their topics? Do they reflect on their strategies for topic selection?
- Are they influenced by what they have read, by others' topics and by past experiences?
- Are they willing to try new forms and new topics?

Examine pupils' writing folders:

- Are they well-organized?
- Does the writing cover a range and variety of topics and forms?
- How often do pupils bring pieces to a conclusion? How often do they begin and then abandon topics?
- What do they do when they have a problem?
- Is there evidence of proofreading and self-correction?
- Have they polished pieces for publication?

Select several pieces of a pupil's writing in different stages of development and across varied forms. An evaluation conference with the writer may indicate which pieces are the most revealing. Analyze and evaluate strategies and the use of the cue systems. A full evaluation includes observations made during writing and in response to coaching.

PROGRESS TOWARD LITERACY

Examine pupils' choices of reading materials over time:

— Are they choosing longer selections?
— Are they investigating a variety of forms and genres?
— Are their choices more challenging in terms of vocabulary and concepts?
— Are they choosing to read more often, taking books home and discussing them with others?
— Are they more willing and able to engage in reading conferences and to discuss text?

Examine pupils' writing in depth:

— Are pupils choosing more suitable and interesting writing topics?
— How well do they follow through on their initial ideas?
— Are they becoming aware of the needs of their readers?
— Are they editing?
— When are they editing—as they go or when they have completed a first draft?
— Are their editing strategies expanding in number and type?
— Do they proofread?
— Can they discuss their writing?
— Do they choose to write?

Consider the development in pupils' use of the cue systems in both reading and writing:

— Are pupils developing fluency, flexibility and problem-solving strategies?
— Do they reread for clarity and meaning?
— Do they regularly monitor and self-correct their reading and writing?
— Does their work reflect the help they receive during coaching and conferences?

Review pupils' Reading Record forms. Observe the scope, duration and the frequency of their reading. Note the commitments and strategies pupils have recorded in the *Comments* column:

— Are they useful?
— Have pupils carried them to completion?

Compare these records with the information you have noted on your record forms:

— Do they seem accurate and complete?

Review pupils' Writing Record forms. Consider the number of pieces attempted and completed, and the scope and variety of topics and purposes:

— Are they writing more often?
— Are their pieces longer and more elaborate?
— Are their graphophonic strategies developing?
— Are their commitments realistic?
— Are pupils becoming accountable for certain strategies?

Compare these records with the information you have noted on your record form:

— Do they seem accurate and complete?

Evaluating Teaching

When we see pupils developing strategies and responding positively, then we know our program in general, and our coaching in particular, must be working. But when pupils are not progressing as well as we expect them to, then we must reflect on the principles set out on page 7 and the consistency of their implementation.

Each principle raises certain questions. Let's consider one pupil's progress in terms of some of these questions, and then consider how and where his program may need adjusting.

1. Does he respond easily to peers within his group, to teachers and to activities? Does he risk trying new strategies, broaching new topics and revealing his thinking? Should we teach him on his own rather than in a group? We reflect on the setting and consider its effect on his comfort and motivation.

2. Is he meaningfully immersed in literacy? Does he participate in demonstrations and group activities? We consider what more we can do to capture his interest and participation.
3. We reflect on the choice and arrangement of reading materials. Does he choose reading materials suitable to his ability and interests? Can he easily access them? Does he choose writing topics that are within his experience? Does he develop them to their conclusion? We consider our coaching strategies.
4. We review Reading Miscue Records and samples of writing. Do we have sufficient and varied examples to reveal his strategies? We identify our specific concerns. We clarify their nature by observing before, during and after reading and writing.
5. Does he pursue meaning as he reads? Does he write to communicate? We reflect on our responses. Do we always respond to, and develop, meaning first? Do our actions match our words? What else can we do to persuade him that meaning is the first priority?
6. Can we identify patterns in his thinking? Does he attempt new strategies? Does he correct himself as he reads and writes? We consider our coaching responses. Do we give him enough time and encouragement? Are we helping him build on his strengths? Do we accept and applaud all evidence of thinking?
7. Does he produce functional representations of reading and writing? Is he becoming more independent? We reflect on our coaching. Do we recognize his strategies? Do we acknowledge and respect what he *can* do? Do we encourage control over his own learning?
8. We reexamine successive examples of his work to identify signs of progress. We consider our coaching priorities in light of his development.
9. We make more observations. We collect baseline data, add to it at regular intervals and reevaluate his progress. We try not to be swayed by comparisons with the progress of others.

We must recognize the positive strategies that pupils at risk bring to their learning. Then we can applaud and confirm their use. Our appreciation lets them know they are on the right track. It also helps them feel good about themselves. Once they become confident learners, then indeed they are well on their way to literacy.

. . . .

REFERENCES

Altwerger, B., Edelsky, C. & B. Flores. "Whole Language: What's New?" In *The Reading Teacher*. Vol. 41, no. 2, 1987.

Atwell, N. *In the Middle: Writing, Reading, and Learning with Adolescents*. Montclair, New Jersey: Boynton-Cook, 1987.

Calkins, L.M. *Living Between the Lines*. Portsmouth, New Hampshire: Heinemann, 1991.

Chow, M., Dobson, L., Hurst, M. & J. Nucich. *Whole Language: Practical Ideas*. Toronto, Ontario: Pippin Publishing, 1991.

Clay, M.M. *Becoming Literate: The Construction of Inner Control*. Portsmouth, New Hampshire: Heinemann, 1991.

Cowley, Joy. *A Monster Sandwich. Storybox* series. Auckland: Shortland, 1983.

Cowley, Joy. *The Sunflower That Went Flop. Storybox* series. Auckland: Shortland, 1982.

Cowley, Joy. *Who Will Be My Mother? Storybox* series. Auckland: Shortland, 1982.

Dobson, L.N. & M.E. Hurst. *How Do Young Children Learn to Read and Write When Meaning Is the Major Focus?* Vancouver: Educational Research Institute of British Columbia, Report No. 86, 1985.

Dobson, L.N. "Connections in Learning to Write and Read: A Study of Children's Development through Kindergarten and First Grade." In J. Mason, Ed., *Reading and Writing Connections*. Needham Heights, Massachusetts: Allyn & Bacon, 1989.

Gentry, J.R. "An Analysis of Developmental Spelling in GNYS AT WORK." In *The Reading Teacher*. Vol. 35, no. 2, 1982.

Goodman, K. "Reading: The Key Is in Children's Language." In *The Reading Teacher*. Vol. 25, no. 6, 1972.

Goodman, Y.M. & C.L. Burke. *Reading Miscue Inventory Manual: Procedure for Diagnosis and Evaluation*. New York: Macmillan, 1972.

Graves, D.H. *Writing: Teachers and Children at Work*. Portsmouth, New Hampshire: Heinemann, 1983.

Hall, N. *The Emergence of Literacy*. Portsmouth, New Hampshire: Heinemann, 1987.

Henderson, E.H. & J.W. Beers, eds. *Developmental and Cognitive Aspects of Learning to Spell: A Reflection of Word Knowledge*. Newark, Delaware: International Reading Association, 1980.

Hurst, M., Dobson, L., Chow, M., Nucich, J., Stickley, L. and G. Smith. *A Program to Foster Literacy: Early Steps in Learning to Write*. Vancouver: B.C. Teachers' Federation, Lesson Aids Service, 1993.

Jaggar, A. & T.M. Smith-Burke, eds. *Observing the Language Learner*. Newark, Delaware: International Reading Association, 1985.

Kotcher, Jean. "Teaching Literacy Through Interaction." Master's thesis. Vancouver: University of British Columbia, 1989.

Martin, B., Jr. *Brown Bear, Brown Bear, What Do You See?* New York: Holt Rinehart & Winston, 1970.

Melser, June. *Little Red Hen*. In *Help Me*. *Storybox* series. Auckland: Shortland, 1980.

Mickelson, N. "Recasting Evaluation: Centred in the Classroom." In *Teacher: Newsmagazine of the B.C. Teachers' Federation*. Vol. 2, no. 3, 1989.

Nucich, Joy E. "An In-Depth Analysis of the Connections Between the Development of Letter-Sound Correspondence in Writing and Beginning Reading." Master's thesis. Vancouver: University of British Columbia, 1991.

Read, C. "Preschool Children's Knowledge of English Phonology." In *Harvard Educational Review*. Vol. 41, no. 1, 1971.

Routman, Regie. *Transitions: From Literature to Literacy*. Portsmouth, New Hampshire: Heinemann, 1988.

Smith, F. *Reading Without Nonsense*. New York: Teachers College Press, 1979.

Strickland, D.S. & L.M. Morrow, eds. *Emerging Literacy: Young Children Learn to Read and Write*. Newark, Delaware: International Reading Association, 1989.

Weaver, C. *Reading Process and Practice: from Socio-psycholinguistics to Whole Language*, second edition. Portsmouth, New Hampshire: Heinemann, 1994.

THE PIPPIN TEACHER'S LIBRARY

The titles in this series are designed to provide a forum for interpreting, in clear, straightforward language, current issues and trends affecting education. Teachers are invited to share — in their own voice — the insights, wisdom and knowledge they have developed out of their professional experiences.

Submissions for publication are welcomed. Manuscripts and proposals will be reviewed by members of the Pippin Teacher's Library Editorial Advisory Board, chaired by Lee Gunderson, PhD, of the University of British Columbia.

Written submissions should be directed to:
The Editorial Director
Pippin Publishing Corporation
85 Ellesmere Road
Suite 232
Toronto, Ontario
Canada
M1R 4B9